6.94

The New
Enchantment of America
VIRGINIA

By Allan Carpenter

CHILDRENS PRESS, CHICAGO

ACKNOWLEDGMENTS

For assistance in the preparation of the revised edition, the author thanks:
MARSHALL MURDAUGH, Commissioner Virginia State Travel Service and MARY SKINNER, Director of Publications, Virginia State Travel Service.

American Airlines—Anne Vitaliano, Director of Public Relations; *Capitol Historical Society,* Washington, D. C.; *Newberry Library,* Chicago, Dr. Lawrence Towner, Director; *Northwestern University Library*, Evanston, Illinois; *United Airlines*—John P. Grember, Manager of Special Promotions; Joseph P. Hopkins, Manager, News Bureau.

UNITED STATES GOVERNMENT AGENCIES: *Department of Agriculture*—Robert Hailstock, Jr., Photography Division, Office of Communication; Donald C. Schuhart, Information Division, Soil Conservation Service. *Army*—Doran Topolosky, Public Affairs Office, Chief of Engineers, Corps of Engineers. *Department of Interior*—Louis Churchville, Director of Communications; EROS Space Program—Phillis Wiepking, Community Affairs; Charles Withington, Geologist; Mrs. Ruth Herbert, Information Specialist; Bureau of Reclamation; National Park Service—Fred Bell and the individual sites; Fish and Wildlife Service—Bob Hines, Public Affairs Office. *Library of Congress*—Dr. Alan Fern, Director of the Department of Research; Sara Wallace, Director of Publications; Dr. Walter W. Ristow, Chief, Geography and Map Division; Herbert Sandborn, Exhibits Officer. *National Archives*—Dr. James B. Rhoads, Archivist of the United States; Albert Meisel, Assistant Archivist for Educational Programs; David Eggenberger, Publications Director; Bill Leary, Still Picture Reference; James Moore, Audio-Visual Archives. *United States Postal Service*—Herb Harris, Stamps Division.

For assistance in the preparation of the first edition, the author thanks:
Ray Hiner, Jr., Supervisor of History, Richmond Public Schools; Division of Industrial Development and Planning; Department of Conservation and Economic Development; Department of Highways; Department of Agriculture and Immigration; Virginia State Chamber of Commerce.

Illustrations on the preceding pages:
Cover photograph: Militia Review at Williamsburg, United Air Lines, Inc.
Page 1: Commemorative stamps of historic interest
Pages 2-3: Blue Ridge Parkway, USDI NPS
Page 3: (Map) USDI Geological Survey
Pages 4-5: Norfolk and Virginia Beach Area, EROS Space Photo, USDI Geological Survey, EROS Data Center

Project Editor, Revised Edition:
  Joan Downing
Assistant Editor, Revised Edition:
  Mary Reidy

Library of Congress Cataloging in Publication Data

Carpenter, John Allan, 1917-
  Virginia.

  (His The new enchantment of America)
  SUMMARY: Discusses the history, natural resources, places of interest, and famous citizens of the Old Dominion state.
  1. Virginia—Juvenile literature.
  [1. Virginia] I. Title.
  II. Series.
  F226.3.C37   1978   975.5   78-8002
  ISBN 0-516-04146-0

Contents

Right: George and Martha Washington in Later Life with their Family, *by Edward Savage.* *Below: Mt. Vernon, home of the Washingtons.*

A True Story to Set the Scene

Colonel George Washington was hurrying to Williamsburg in May of 1758. Crossing the Pamunkey River he met Colonel Richard Chamberlayne, who invited him to dinner at his home, Poplar Grove. Washington declined, stating that the dispatches he was carrying would not permit him to linger even for a moment. But then Colonel Chamberlayne made a statement that immediately attracted the young Washington, soon to be a hero of the French and Indian War. If Washington stayed for dinner, Colonel Chamberlayne promised, he would meet "the prettiest and richest widow in Virginia."

Washington quickly gave in; he agreed to "dine—only dine"; by "borrowing of the night" he might reach Williamsburg the next morning.

While his faithful servant, Bishop, held his master's dashing horse, Washington remained inside, captivated by the charms of the pretty widow, Martha Dandridge Custis. Finally Colonel Chamberlayne said that no guest of his left his home at such a late hour, and Washington stayed the night.

On other trips to the area he visited with Martha Custis at her splendid estate, called the White House. Only two months after their first meeting, Colonel Washington was addressing his letters "to one whose life is now inseparable from mine. Since that happy hour when we made our pledges to each other, my thoughts have been continually going to you as to another self."

George Washington and Martha Custis were married in January of 1759, after the French and Indian War diminished. The exact date and location of the wedding are unknown, although it probably was on January 6 at the bride's White House estate.

Many years later Martha's grandson spoke to a servant of his grandmother who had reached a hundred years of age: "And so you remember when Colonel Washington came a courting of your mistress?"

"Ay, master, that I do, great times, sir, great times! . . ." Of Washington the ancient servant said, "Never the likes of him . . .

so tall, so straight and then he sat a horse and rode with such an air! Ah, sir; he was like no one else! Many of the grandest gentlemen in their gold lace were at the wedding, but none looked like the man himself!"

A rare old account describes the bride's wedding dress: "A white satin quilt, over which a heavy white silk, interwoven with threads of silver, was looped back with white satin ribbons, richly brocaded in a leaf pattern. Her bodice was of plain satin, and the brocade was fastened on the bust with a stiff butterfly bow of the ribbon. Delicate lace finished the low, square neck. There were close elbow sleeves revealing a puff and frill of lace. Strings of pearls were woven in and out of her powdered hair. Her high-heeled slippers were of white satin, with brilliant buckles."

The couple spent their honeymoon in Williamsburg, while the groom took his place in the House of Burgesses and the bride closed her town house at Williamsburg. When the session of the House ended, the Washingtons immediately went to Mount Vernon, Washington's home on the Potomac River.

When Washington left his beloved estate again, sixteen years later, he began a course that would establish a new country, one that would become one of the greatest in the family of nations.

The story of George Washington and his pretty dinner partner is one of the many stories of the enchantment of Virginia. And it has in it many of the things which are so typical of the history of the Old Dominion—famous and wealthy people, handsome plantations, courtly hospitality, and romance.

Washington's study in Mt. Vernon.

Lay of the Land

HONOR TO THE VIRGIN QUEEN

In 1497 British explorer John Cabot made an extended voyage along the northern shoreline of North America. Years later, because of this exploration, eager ministers of Queen Elizabeth I claimed for Her Majesty all the vast region north of the lands claimed by the Spanish. In honor of Elizabeth, called the Virgin Queen, they named the entire region Virginia.

At one time this huge empire was considered to include most of the present-day United States east of the Mississippi River. Although the Virginia of the present has shrunk from this once tremendous area, the state can still look back proudly to being the "Mother of the States."

VIRGINIA TODAY

Virginia today covers 40,815 square miles (105,710 square kilometers), including 977 square miles (2,530 square kilometers), of inland water surface. Much of this water area is made up of the fat fingers of water called *estuaries* which reach far inland from the sea. The greatest of these is Chesapeake Bay. Others of these great "drowned river valleys" are the estuaries of the James, York, and Rappahannock rivers. The estuary of the Potomac River is not within the boundaries of Virginia, since the state boundary is set south of the Potomac's waterline.

These great estuaries cut Virginia's mainland into three parallel peninsulas. Across Chesapeake Bay is another peninsula—Virginia's portion of the Delmarva Peninsula (shared by Delaware, Maryland, and Virginia). The Virginia portion is itself a smaller peninsula jutting off from the larger one.

Virginia is drained by nine major rivers: the Potomac, Rappahannock, York, James, Chowan, Roanoke, New (in spite of its name one of the oldest on the continent), Tennessee, and Big Sandy. The last three flow to the north and west and eventually reach the Mississippi; for that reason they are called Virginia's "western waters."

Three great river systems—the Rappahannock, York, and James—flow almost their entire courses within the state. The James cuts a 4-mile (6.4-kilometer) opening through the Blue Ridge Mountains to empty into Chesapeake Bay instead of the Ohio River system. The Roanoke River flows across Virginia for 240 miles (386 kilometers) before entering North Carolina. Other large Virginia rivers are the Clinch, Holston, and Powell.

The "portals" of Chesapeake Bay consist of Cape Charles on the north and Cape Henry on the south. Where the waters of the Nansemond, James, and Elizabeth rivers empty into Chesapeake Bay is one of the world's finest natural harbors—Hampton Roads. This is just a part of the huge 3,315-mile (5,300-kilometer) tidal shoreline of Virginia.

The state's major lakes were all made by human engineering. They include Smith Mountain Lake, Philpott Reservoir, Claytor Lake, Lessville Lake, and parts of Buggs Island Lake and Lake Gaston. These latter two are shared with North Carolina.

Virginia's neighbor states are Maryland, West Virginia, Kentucky, Tennessee, and North Carolina. Geographers divide Virginia into five main land areas known as *physiographic provinces*—Coastal Plain (Tidewater), Piedmont, Blue Ridge, Valley and Ridge, and Appalachian Plateau.

Between the Coastal Plain and the Piedmont is the Fall Line. The major rivers can be navigated to this line. The Blue Ridge is the highest section of the state—a kind of craggy backbone. The western and northern portions of the state are seamed and creased with other rows of parallel mountain systems and valleys. One of the most famous valleys in the United States—whose name is known to almost everyone through song and story—is the Shenandoah Valley. The tallest peak in Virginia is Mount Rogers, in the extreme southwest, rising to 5,729 feet (1,746 meters).

Where Virginia's westward-aimed "dart" comes to its sharp point is White Top Mountain; there the three states of Kentucky, Virginia,

12

Left: Virginia's Natural Bridge is one of America's best-known geographic features. Below: Natural Chimneys at Mt. Solon, Virginia, is an unusual geographic formation.

and Tennessee come together at famed Cumberland Gap. Cumberland Gap is twenty-five miles (forty kilometers) farther west than Detroit, making part of Virginia "mid-western."

IN THE DISTANT PAST

Many times, in a far, far distant past, much of what is now Virginia west of the Blue Ridge was flooded by ancient seas. Then the shrinking of the earth squeezed enormous folds of the rocky layers of the earth into the air, forming the ancestors of today's Appalachian Mountains.

Over ages of time, wind and water wore these great ranges almost level. Then they were raised up again, eroded down, and raised a third time. The present Appalachians, including the Blue Ridge, Shenandoah, and Allegheny mountains, are probably eight hundred million years old, among the oldest mountains on the earth's surface. If the earth lasts long enough, they probably will be worn down once more to the level of the land around them.

Dinosaur footprints in Loudoun County, whales' teeth, portions of ancient elephants, and the fossil plants that made Virginia's coal fields are among the traces left of the living things of ancient times.

CLIMATE

Even in midsummer Virginia temperatures are moderate, and cool in the mountains. In midwinter, heavy or long-lasting snow is rare. Precipitation, averaging 45 inches (114 centimeters) per year, is spread throughout the months. Spring comes early and stays late. By late April gardens are magnificent. Even before that, the long wildflower parade has begun. Autumn is equally long and delightful. In the mountains, it turns the great hardwood forests into a breathtaking kaleidoscope of color. In Virginia's Tidewater, the best of summer lingers late, with ocean swimming possible generally well into October.

Footsteps on the Land

OF "GRAVE AND MAJESTICALL COUNTENANCE"

Just before the coming of the first Europeans to the Virginia region, one of the most distinctive and unusual Indian civilizations of what is now the United States had its headquarters there.

The greatest part of Virginia's land was ruled by Wahunsonacock, or Powhatan, as the English called him. His abilities in war and diplomacy had enabled him to weld a confederacy of thirty separate kingdoms under his autocratic rule. The confederacy included as many as 161 villages, with an army of 2,400 trained warriors. These people spoke an Algonquin language stock, one of the three main native language groups in what is now Virginia.

King Powhatan ruled from thirty-six different tribal capitals, in each of which he had a royal house. The empire of Powhatan was subdivided into parts, each ruled by a civil leader known as a *sachem* and a war leader, a *werowance*. Leaders were advised by the priests and a group of leaders known as the tribal council. Each division had its capital, or seat of government.

When British Captain John Smith first visited the principal Indian capital of Werowocomoco, he wrote that he found the "Emperor proudly lying upon a Bedstead a foote high, upon tenn or twelve mattes, richly hung with manie Chaynes of great Pearles about necke, and covered with great Covering of *Rahaughcums*. At [his] head sat a woman, at his feete another; on each side sitting upon a Matte uppon the ground, were raunged his chiefe men on each side the fire, tenne in a ranke, and behinde them as many yong women, each [with] a great Chaine of white Beades over their shoulders, their heades painted in redde: and [Powhatan] with such a grave Majesticall countenance, as drave me into admiration...."

Other peoples in Virginia were the tribes of Sioux stock, living generally in what is now north-central Virginia, and the Iroquois tribes. Some of the Sioux tribes were grouped into what is known as the Monacan Confederacy. Most of the Iroquois tribes did not make permanent homes in present Virginia, but they tried to extend the

A 1585 map of Virginia by James White. The coat of arms is Sir Walter Raleigh, who named the region in honor of Elizabeth I, "The Virgin Queen."

authority of the Iroquois Confederacy ever farther southward. The Rickohockan group and other Cherokee-related groups are usually identified with the Iroquois, and they lived in the mountain regions of the present state.

The villages, houses, clothing, crafts, hunting, agriculture, and religion of the Indians in what is now Virginia were generally similar to those of other eastern regions. One of the more interesting customs was the "sweating house," heated with red-hot stones. It resembled the Finnish sauna, popular in the modern United States.

Another unique custom was the manner of burial of the chiefs. The leader's dead body was disemboweled and stuffed with sand, then wrapped and laid in the temple where it dried, mummylike.

Virginia also had many other small tribes scattered through its lands.

Comparatively little is known about the people who lived in Virginia before the first Europeans arrived. Some of the ancient mounds, such as Hayes Creek, and other remains, such as the stone implement quarries near New Hampden, have been examined. Many relics of early periods are exhibited in museums throughout the state. An Indian mound near Ruckersville was described by Thomas Jefferson in his *Notes on Virginia.*

A TOWN FOR JAMES THE KING

Historians are not certain who the first European visitor to Virginia really was. Some of the early explorers of North America certainly passed by, and might have set foot in the present state. Both the English and Spanish laid claim to the region, and as early as the 1580s Spanish Jesuit missionaries had set up a mission on the banks of Aquia Creek in the Potomac region. Before the missionaries could attempt to convert the Indians to Christianity, however, they were massacred by the Indians. Soldiers were sent north by the Spaniards to avenge the killing of their religious men, and the Indians long remembered their violent deeds.

In 1606 King James I of England chartered two companies to colonize Virginia. The London Company was to colonize Virginia south of Chesapeake Bay and the Plymouth Company to colonize northern Virginia (roughly everything north of Chesapeake Bay).

On April 26, 1607, three little ships, the *Discovery,* the *Godspeed,* and the flagship *Susan Constant,* landed at what is now Virginia Beach. Their people set up a cross to show their thankfulness at arriving in the New World. They named the place where they landed Cape Henry and the opposite cape of this huge mouth of the ocean Cape Charles, to honor the king's sons. Here they opened the sealed instructions they had carried across the ocean, to find what the London Company required them to do in their new land.

They moved slowly up the great Chesapeake Bay, and on the evening of May 14, 1607, the little ships were, according to their own account, "moored to the trees in 6 fathoms of water," off an island in the river. That night, as a forecast of difficulties in the future, the Indians came "creeping upon all foures from the Hills, like Beares, with their Bowes in their mouthes."

The next morning the very first Virginians, 104 in number, went ashore and "set to work about the fortification." They built a tiny fort and inside they constructed a chapel, some huts with thatched roofs, and a storehouse. In honor of the king, they named the little settlement James Towne, later Jamestown.

This was to become the first permanent English settlement in America.

When the colonists landed, one of the men was in chains for some minor cause. This was John Smith. However, when the colonists opened their sealed orders it was found that Smith was to be one of the members of the governing council, so he was freed. Gradually Smith became the acknowledged leader.

A large number of the colonists considered themselves "gentlemen" and too dignified for ordinary labor. There was much bickering over what ought to be done. Smith persuaded a number of them to work. When blisters appeared on their hands they began to swear, so at this point Smith threatened to pour pitchers of cold water down their sleeves if they continued their swearing.

John Smith was captured by Indians later in the year and taken to Powhatan's capital of Werowocomoco. This was the scene of one of the world's most famous stories but no one knows for sure whether the story is true. Powhatan is said to have ordered Smith beheaded, but just before the executioner brought his hatchet down, a beautiful young Indian girl threw her body over Smith to protect him and save his life. This was the thirteen-year-old Princess Pocahontas, daughter of Powhatan. It is probably true that she saved Smith from death, even if not in such a romantic manner.

Not long after, Smith persuaded Powhatan to trade supplies much needed by the colonists for some glass beads and other trinkets. King James was so impressed by the colonists' description of Powhatan's power that he ordered the colonists to crown him a king.

Powhatan refused to go to Jamestown, so the colonists held the ceremony of coronation in his own capital. Later, when the colonists needed more supplies, the king demanded and got a European-type house in return. This house remained standing until 1915.

The teen-aged Pocahontas often visited Jamestown, where she flitted about merrily and entertained the settlers by turning cartwheels around the walls of the stockade. She was fascinated by Captain Smith, and apparently fell madly in love with him, but he ignored her.

In October of 1609 Captain John Smith returned to England for medical treatment of severe injuries. The London Company had never sent enough supplies for the colony's needs, and most of the settlers sent by the company did not know how to do useful work. Smith wrote a letter, known as his "rude letter," to the company, saying, "When you send againe I entreat you rather send but thirty Carpenters, husbandmen, gardiners, fishermen, blacksmiths, masons and diggers up of trees, roots, well provided; than a thousand of such as we have: for except wee be able both to lodge them and feed them, the most will consume with want of necessaries before they can be made good for anything."

The winter of 1609-1610 became known as the "starving time." Food was almost gone; the region was unhealthy and many took sick. When the winter started, the colony numbered five hundred; by May only sixty-five miserable survivors were left. They abandoned Jamestown and started for England. At Mulberry Island, only fourteen miles (twenty-two kilometers) away, they met Lord De la Warr, who had come from England with supplies and new settlers. Encouraged by this, the survivors turned back.

PROGRESS

In the next few years, the English colony began to rebuild. The Indians had become more resentful and began to mount attacks against the colonists. By 1614 John Rolfe had become the leader of the colony. He promoted the growing of tobacco, which proved to be a successful crop, much in demand in England. He also married Princess Pocahontas, who had been brought to Jamestown as a

19

hostage. After the marriage, Rolfe's father-in-law, Powhatan, kept his people generally quiet until his death in 1618.

In 1619, it appeared that the colony might succeed. It was divided into eleven regularly established plantations, including several settlements such as Henricopolis (or Henricus). Henry Hamor, colonial secretary, described the town as having three streets, houses, a small church, and the beginnings of a larger one. Five blockhouses had been built along the river and their residents guarded the town from attack.

In 1619 occurred three of the most significant events of our country's history. An election was held to choose two representatives from each of the eleven plantations of the colony to form a "House of Burgesses." This became the first democratically elected legislative body in the New World. As the Virginia legislature today, it has now become the oldest continuously operating legislative body in the Western Hemisphere. Also in 1619 the colony was organized into four "incorporations" or major divisions, resembling the later counties.

Another event of that year was the arrival of the first European women and the first blacks, from a Dutch ship. These blacks, however, were not to be slaves but came in as indentured servants, who would be free after a time of service.

A PERIOD OF TROUBLE

After the death of Powhatan, Indian rule in the region was taken over by King Opechancanough. He pretended friendship with the settlers, but laid careful plans to drive them from the country. Opechancanough instructed his followers to attack at a particular hour on March 22, 1622, along a 140-mile (225-kilometer) front covering most of the colonized area.

In this attack 347 colonists lost their lives. The Indian plan might have succeeded completely, but Jamestown was saved by Chanco, an Indian youth who had been converted to the Christian religion by the colonists. He warned the colonists of the coming attack.

Many years passed before Virginia was able to recover from this massacre. Plans for setting up schools and universities to convert the Indians to Christianity and give them a European education were abandoned. A six-mile-long (nearly ten kilometers) palisade was built across the peninsula as protection against Indian attack.

The last great Indian uprising in eastern Virginia came in 1644. Aged Opechancanough made a final desperate effort but failed. Two years later the king was captured by a force under Governor William Berkeley and carried wounded on a stretcher to Jamestown. There he was shot by a soldier who was supposed to have been guarding him. The mightiest Indian empire north of Mexico had been made powerless.

SEEDS OF FREEDOM

The London Company charter had been revoked in 1624. By this time Virginia was ruled as a royal colony. However, there was a growing independence in the colony. King Charles I had recognized the House of Burgesses in 1628, and as early as 1635 the House of Burgesses had been able to cause the removal of one royal governor.

Forty years later there was an even more important revolt against royal government. Sir William Berkeley had been away from the governorship for some years when he was selected again in 1660 by the Burgesses. Over the years, he became more interested in being powerful and less interested in the people he governed.

In 1674 Nathaniel Bacon began to rally the people against the governor, who had refused to defend the western frontiers against Indian attack. More and more followers joined him. Although Berkeley called him "the greatest rebel that ever was in Virginia," he was forced to pardon him. Later Bacon virtually took over the government, and Berkeley fled to the eastern shore.

When Berkeley returned to Jamestown, Bacon and his followers attacked the town and set it on fire. Then Bacon wrote what has come to be known as "America's first declaration of independence." In his proclamation Bacon declared that if the king of Eng-

Nathaniel Bacon, Jr., confronts Sir William Berkeley
before the Statehouse at Jamestown, 1676, *by Sidney E. King.*

land upheld Berkeley, the people of Virginia would have to fight for
their liberties or leave the colony. He started off on a trip around
Virginia to persuade people to stand firm, but he died of a fever on
the trip.

After Bacon's death, Berkeley hanged twenty of Bacon's leaders
without trial and took over the property of many others. On hearing
of this, King Charles II wrote, "That old fool has hanged more men
in that naked country than I have done here for the murder of my
father."

However, Bacon's stirring message had aroused Virginians so
much that a hundred years later they were perhaps better prepared to
declare their independence from England than was any other American colony.

The years that followed were a period of exploration, with the
frontier pushing westward, and of growth and development. It was a
time of pirates and finally the destruction of most of them, of
authorizing ports, and of treaties with the Indians. In 1699
Williamsburg, named in honor of King William III, was made the
capital.

PLANTATION LIFE

In 1716 pleasure-loving Governor Alexander Spotswood led an expedition to the west, looking for a new pass over the mountains. Carrying a large supply of almost every wine and liquor known, the governor and his merry party drank toasts on practically every occasion. When the explorers returned, the governor had miniature golden horseshoes made and covered with jewels; he gave each member of his party one of these emblems, and the men became known as "Knights of the Golden Horsehoe."

By the time Governor Spotswood retired in 1722, he had acquired 85,000 acres (34,400 hectares) of land. He lived like a king on his estate, which was decorated with terraced gardens and a marble fountain. He had little concern about entertaining four hundred people for dinner, even on short notice.

Governor Spotswood was not alone in his luxurious living. In Virginia the plantation system reached a peak of wealth, cultivated manners, and elegant living. Each plantation was almost like a self-sufficient little world presided over by its owners.

In the spring, tulips and jonquils line the mall of the George Wythe House, which still shows the glamor of plantation life.

Thomas Lord Fairfax inherited from his mother the proprietary of Northern Neck, a vast estate of five million acres (over two million hectares), including all the land between the Rappahannock and Potomac rivers. This was the largest estate in Virginia, though there were others almost as big.

In 1649 Denbigh Plantation, owned by Samuel Mathews, grew hemp and flax, tanned leather and made shoes, and raised dairy cattle, pigs, and poultry. Stratford Plantation was also very wealthy. The owner, Philip Ludwell Lee, had a band of musicians available at all times to his daughters, Matilda and Flora, for dancing. The land on nearly all of Virginia's plantations was extremely rich and fertile.

Of course, the vast number of Virginians of those days were far less fortunate. The wealth of the plantations was built on the unceasing labor of the slaves, who had almost no hope of a different life. Much of the life of the plantations depended on the slaves, many of whom were skilled servants and artisans who provided the decorations, food and drink, and other wants of the plantation owners. There were some free blacks, who in some ways had a more difficult time than the slaves. Many small white landholders, merchants, shopkeepers, artisans, tradesmen, and the "common" people often had little hope in life.

EYES ON THE FRONTIER

During the first half of the 1700s the frontier had been pushing westward. In 1738 Augusta County was formed. On paper this enormous tract extended from the Blue Ridge to the Mississippi and from the Great Lakes to North Carolina.

Since this land was also claimed by the French, there was growing trouble as the English moved in. The French encouraged the Indians to attack English settlers. These difficulties at last grew into what we know as the French and Indian War.

This war brought to prominence a young Virginia officer and aristocrat named George Washington. He did much to save the British from defeat in the wilderness of Pennsylvania and Maryland. For

Virginia's defense Washington built Fort Loudoun, near present Winchester. The French felt it could never be captured. After demonstrating his ability in many ways, Washington was named commander-in-chief of the royal forces in Virginia, the first of the long series of high honors that would be his.

The Indian wars brought much terror and suffering to the people of the frontier. One of the strange experiences of the period was that of the Brubakers, who lived near present Luray. One evening Mrs. Brubaker had a vision that Indians would attack. It was so vivid that she could count the number of Indians as they were camped on a nearby mountain. Her vision showed that they would attack the next morning, and she persuaded her husband to take the family to a place where they could be safe. Their neighbors, the Stones, made fun of this prophecy, but the attack took place just as Mrs. Brubaker had foretold; Stone was killed, and his family carried off as captives.

Although the French and Indian War was officially ended by 1763, attacks continued through much of the Revolutionary War.

PRELUDE TO FREEDOM

In order to pay the expenses of the French and Indian War, the British government placed "stamp" taxes on several kinds of items used in the colonies. The Virginia General Assembly passed the "Virginia Resolves," which pointed out the injustice in placing taxes on the colonies when they had no voice in the law. The most notable leader in calling for the Virginia Resolves was young Patrick Henry, who stirred tremendous excitement when he roared, "Caesar had his Brutus, Charles I his Cromwell, and George III——" At this point many feared the youthful orator might be accused of treason, but he ended safely and cleverly by saying, "may profit from their example." This has been called the "first frank challenge to the King."

The Stamp Taxes were repealed, but after a year other taxes were levied and dissatisfaction grew in Virginia and the other colonies. In 1773, a group of Virginians, including Thomas Jefferson, Richard Henry Lee, Patrick Henry, and George Mason, persuaded the

Virginia General Assembly to set up a Committee of Correspondence to work with the other colonies to protect their interests.

The hated taxes were repealed, except for the tax on tea, but this failed to satisfy the colonists. Virginia had its own "tea party," as did the other colonies, destroying tea rather than paying British taxes on it. The First Continental Congress was organized, and Peyton Randolph of Virginia was chosen as its president.

Although haughty Governor John Murray Dunmore had dissolved the Virginia General Assembly, Virginians met in several conventions. At the second convention Patrick Henry in a fiery speech called for the arming of the militia as he orated, "Gentlemen may cry 'Peace! Peace!' but there is no peace. The war is actually begun! . . . Is life so dear or peace so sweet as to be purchased at the price of chains and slavery? Forbid it, Almighty God! I know not what course others may take," and then he closed with the familiar words, "but, as for me, give me liberty, or give me death!"

When Governor Dunmore took the public gunpowder from the arsenal, Patrick Henry organized a small army and forced the governor to pay for the powder. Lord Dunmore declared Henry to be an outlaw and the governor later fled to a warship.

On June 15, 1775, Virginia's own George Washington accepted the call of the Continental Congress as commander-in-chief of all American forces. He hurried to Boston to take command of his untrained troops. The scene had been set for revolution.

Patrick Henry harangues the House of Burgesses in protest of the Stamp Act. *Painting by Peter Rothermel.*

Yesterday and Today

FROM BOSTON TO YORKTOWN

The first armed clash of the Revolutionary War in Virginia took place at Great Bridge on December 9, 1775, when Virginia militia defeated Lord Dunmore.

On May 6, 1776, the Fifth Virginia Convention meeting at Williamsburg declared the colony to be a free and independent commonwealth. (Virginia is still officially referred to as a commonwealth, rather than as a state.) On June 7, Richard Henry Lee of Virginia suggested to the Continental Congress that it accept a declaration of independence. On June 12, the Virginia convention adopted George Mason's Bill of Rights and then adopted a constitution which lasted more than fifty years. The Virginia bill of rights was later used as a model for the United States Bill of Rights.

In 1778 Virginia played an unusual part in the war by supporting George Rogers Clark as he made the western frontiers safe against the British. The next year Thomas Jefferson succeeded Patrick Henry as Virginia's governor. The war came to Virginia in earnest that year when Sir George Collier sailed into Hampton Roads and raided the countryside around Portsmouth. In 1780 there were raids by General Alexander Leslie and Benedict Arnold.

On May 20, 1781, Lord Charles Cornwallis arrived in Virginia and soon, with seven thousand soldiers, began to pursue General Lafayette, who was defending Virginia. after Lafayette had been joined by General "Mad" Anthony Wayne, they began to push Cornwallis, who finally arrived at Yorktown and fortified it.

Meanwhile, the American forces had been strengthened by three thousand French troops led by Admiral François Joseph Paul de Grasse, and General Washington decided on an all-out effort in Virginia. Washington and the French general Jean Baptiste de Rochambeau were able to bring large numbers of their troops to Virginia in an amazingly short time—one of the great forced marches of history. Admiral de Grasse defeated the British navy and kept it from bringing reinforcements to Lord Charles Cornwallis.

Surrender of Lord Cornwallis at Yorktown,
October 19, 1781. *Painting by John Trumbull.*

The British in Yorktown were completely surrounded and a long
siege began. General Thomas Nelson gladly shelled his own house
when it was occupied by the British. One of the most thrilling
individual actions in the siege and battle occurred when young Colonel Alexander Hamilton stormed and seized an enemy stronghold.

Unable to escape from Yorktown, Cornwallis at last sent his representatives to the Moore house to arrange for his surrender on October 18, 1781. On a broad plain near Yorktown the endless rows of
British soldiers marched out, their red coats gleaming, to lay down
their arms, while a military band blared the appropriate tune, *The
World Turned Upside Down.*

After six years of struggle against seemingly hopeless odds, the
skill and will of General Washington and his many comrades in arms
had achieved final victory for American independence. It seemed fit-
ting that this should occur at Yorktown in his own Virginia.

28

STATEHOOD

In the next six years, the inefficient Articles of Confederation provided rules for governing the newly formed country. In 1787 a group of American leaders met at a convention in Philadelphia. The move to draw up a constitution and form a new government had been encouraged and fostered by many prominent Virginians, including Washington and James Madison. Thomas Jefferson did not take part because at the time he was serving in Europe as an ambassador.

Washington was made president of the convention, and James Madison played a very important role in writing the American Constitution. However, there were many things about the new government that the Virginia delegates did not like. They wanted a bill of rights much like their own and they wanted import of slaves to be stopped immediately, as well as other changes.

Although Virginia wanted at least forty amendments to the new constitution and there was a good deal of opposition among Virginia's delegates to approving the document, it was finally accepted by Virginia in June of 1788.

The Commonwealth of Virginia became the tenth state of the United States of America. George Washington became the first in a historic succession of American Presidents who came from that commonwealth.

GAINS AND SETBACKS

Little more than a year after Virginia joined the Union, it made a generous contribution to the new nation—a sizable tract of land along the Potomac at Alexandria to be used for a new national capital. In 1792 another large tract of land was lopped off when Kentucky, formerly a Virginia county, became a state.

The leadership of Virginia shone in the first years of the new nation as one Virginian after another became President—Washington, Jefferson, Madison, Monroe—a line separated only by the second President, New Englander John Adams.

During the War of 1812, fought between the United States and England, a number of Virginia communities and plantations were attacked and pillaged. However, attempted invasions at Norfolk and Portsmouth were driven off. President Madison and his wife Dolley fled to Virginia to escape the British capture of Washington. Dolley Madison brought with her the things she had been able to save before the White House was burned, including a copy of the Declaration of Independence and a portrait of George Washington.

The period following the war was mainly one of improvement of communications, consolidation, and change within the state. By this time much of Virginia's eastern land had been used up and abandoned, and the western areas were progressing rapidly.

THE GATHERING CLOUDS

It was a Virginia black man, Anthony Johnson, who held the first slave in Virginia. The number of slaves increased greatly, in the nineteenth century. In 1860 there were 52,168 Virginians who held slaves, although many leading Virginians spoke bitterly against the "lifelong ordeal" of slavery. In his first draft of the Declaration of Independence, Thomas Jefferson wrote that the king of England had "waged cruel war against human nature itself, violating its most sacred right of life and liberty in the person of a distant people who never offended him, captivating and carrying them into slavery in another hemisphere." This wording was cut out of the Declaration by South Carolina and Georgia.

Virginia's George Mason refused to sign the Constitution of the United States because it did not condemn slavery. Elizabeth Russell, sister of Patrick Henry, freed her slaves, saying, ". . . that it is both sinful and unjust, as they are by nature equally free as myself, to continue them in slavery." Another Southerner, John Hartwell Cocke, condemned slavery as "the great cause of all the great evils of our lands."

In 1778 Virginia became the first government in the world to make the slave trade a criminal offense. Emancipation of Virginia's black people was almost voted in 1832. An organization called the American Colonization Society was set up to free American slaves and send them to the West African nation of Liberia. The Virginia branch of the society sent 243 free blacks to Liberia in a single year. Liberia's capital, Monrovia, was named in honor of President James Monroe.

Most of Virginia's abolitionists (people who opposed slavery) lived in the state's western section. However, even in the east some risked their safety to help slaves. Shoe dealer James A. Smith shipped Henry Brown to freedom in the North completely encased in a box labeled "shoes." Smith was later caught trying to free two other blacks in the same way and was sent to prison.

However, in spite of some opposition to slavery, the majority of Virginians supported it. Many felt that efforts in the North to do away with slavery were unjustified interference with the South's affairs. Especially in eastern Virginia, large profits were made by those who raised and sold slaves like cattle.

LIKE A STONE WALL

A Virginian, Edmund Riffin, was given the "privilege" of firing the first shot at Fort Sumter, South Carolina, which provided the signal that began the Civil War. When Virginia seceded from the Union on April 17, 1861, "ten thousand hurrahing men and boys carried torches" around Richmond. Fireworks burst above the city, and there was much celebration. Richmond became the capital city of the Confederacy—which was made up of the Southern states that seceded from the United States over the question of slavery—on May 29 of that year.

The South won its first great victory on July 21, 1861, in the Battle of Manassas (Virginia), also known as the first Battle of Bull Run. (Bull Run was the name of the stream that ran through the battlefield.) In this battle General Barnard E. Bee marveled at the courage of one of his fellow officers, Thomas Jonathan Jackson, and gave him a lasting nickname when he exclaimed, "There stands

Jackson like a stone wall." This officer has been known to history ever since as Stonewall Jackson.

Virginia might have been given the same nickname, for she stood like a stone wall in the defense of the Confederacy through four long years. Virginia was the key battleground of the war. The Winchester area alone was the scene of over one hundred engagements and the city of Fredericksburg changed hands seven times. The Shenandoah Valley became known as the "pathway of war."

In early 1862, Union troops occupied Alexandria and also western Virginia (which became the state of West Virginia on June 20, 1863). The South prepared for a great attack from the North. One of the most interesting of these preparations was the converting of the ship *Merrimac* into an iron-covered warship known as the *Virginia*. On March 8, 1862, the *Virginia* sank several Union war ships. On the next day the *Virginia* met the *Monitor,* another new type of boat, nicknamed "a cheesebox on a raft" because of its shape. Through a four-hour period the two ships pounded each other in a battle that is said to have completely altered naval warfare.

Important military movements began on land in Virginia at about the same time. Union General George McClellan began a march on Richmond, and in May he came within sight of the Confederate capital. Norfolk fell to Union forces on May 10, and the Union fleet tried to help the attack on Richmond but was stopped at Drewry's Bluff. One of the great military leaders of all time—Robert Edward Lee—had been placed in command of the Confederate army in Virginia. Lee drove McClellan back from Richmond and saved the Confederate capital.

After this McClellan turned to meet an attack in the Shenandoah Valley. There General Stonewall Jackson carried on a campaign that has been called "a model of military strategy," holding the valley against heavy odds. One of Jackson's most amazing accomplishments was moving 22,000 soldiers in a tremendous march of fifty-six miles (about ninety kilometers) in two days to encircle the Union army.

Union forces marched south again in 1863. At Chancellorsville on May 2 and 3 General Lee defeated the forces of General Joseph

Hooker, forces numbering more than twice his own. However, this was the last of the long series of Union disasters. The South lost its "stone wall" during this battle when General Jackson was shot by his own forces, who did not recognize him in the dusk. Many have said that this was a loss from which the South could never quite recover.

After General Ulysses S. Grant was made Union commander, he and General George G. Meade turned toward Virginia. On May 4 the Wilderness Battle began an eleven-month campaign to decide the fate of Virginia. Beginning May 8, the five-day Battle of Spotsylvania Courthouse brought some of the bloodiest fighting of the entire war.

All attempts by Union forces to break through the defenses of Richmond failed in 1864. Then in the spring of 1865 Grant began his final drive. On April 2 came the first break in General Robert E.

A group at the Fredericksburg and Spotsylvania National Military Park reenact a battle scene.

Lee's line—southwest of Richmond. Although the second line of Richmond's defenses was never conquered, on April 3 Confederate forces and civilians were removed from Petersburg and Richmond.

The next day Richmond was burned by its own people to keep everything useful out of Union hands. For the period of April 3 to April 10, Danville was the capital of the dying Confederacy. Here President Jefferson Davis held the last full meetings of his cabinet.

Grant continued to pursue Lee's forces until April 9. The exhausted, starving, poorly equipped remnants of the once mighty Confederate army, camped near Appomattox Courthouse, saw no other course except surrender.

General Lee found a sparkling new uniform and went to the living room of the Wilmer McLean house near the courthouse. Shortly afterward, General Grant hurried up. To save time, he had rushed in from the field, dusty and unkempt, with no change of uniform. He apologized for his appearance to his old acquaintance, General Lee. Grant may have remembered the occasion during the Mexican War when Lee had reprimanded him for his untidy appearance. The Southern general inquired what surrender terms Grant might offer, and the Northern commander sat down at the same table to write. A deep silence followed, during which only the scratching of Grant's pen could be heard.

General Lee felt that the terms were most generous. The soldiers would not be held as prisoners but would be paroled if they promised not to go to war against the Union. Only the property of the Confederate government or other public property would have to be surrendered. Since nearly all the horses were the property of the soldiers, they would have them for the spring plowing. Grant further ordered his soldiers to supply rations so that the Confederate soldiers need not starve.

When news of the surrender came, Grant's troops were ready for a tremendous victory celebration, but General Grant refused to let them do anything that would make the Confederate forces more bitter. He hoped that in the McLean house and the surrounding area the first steps had been taken to reunite, in a humane way, the separated and brutally suffering nation.

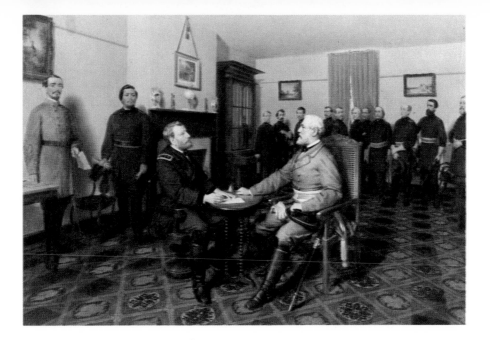

The Surrender of General Lee to General Grant,
April 9, 1865. *Painting by L.M.D. Guillaume.*

AWFUL AFTERMATH

This hope was not to be. With the assassination of President Abraham Lincoln, some who believed the South must pay bitterly for the war felt they had gained their way. For most of the time between the end of the war and 1870, Virginia and the other Southern states were under repressive federal military control. However, attempts were made at various times to regain a civilian government for Virginia.

In July of 1869, Virginia's people voted to approve a new constitution. They rejected clauses that took the vote away from Confederate military officers and prohibited from holding office anyone who had helped the Confederacy. The new legislature met under this constitution and approved the Fourteenth and Fifteenth amendments to the United States Constitution. On January 26, 1870, Virginia once again became a sovereign state. Virginians had some satisfaction in the fact that the "carpetbaggers," who had controlled some of the other Southern states, had not had as much control in the Old Dominion.

But wartime troubles were not over. Most of the wealth of Virginia had been poured into the war effort. Plantations and farms had been left in ruin, without seeds to plant or livestock to raise. Railroads were wrecked or in bad repair. Manufacturing plants had been demolished by Union troops so they could not turn out war supplies, or by the Confederates so they would not fall into Union hands. Private and public debts were so huge that it appeared they could never be repaid. West Virginia, which had become a separate state, refused to pay its share of debts dating before the war. In spite of federal efforts to help newly freed blacks, great numbers of them were in terrible need. They had been cut off from their old life with almost no opportunities to create a better new life.

Turmoil continued as General William Mahone gained great political power in the 1870s and became the most important political figure of the state until 1889. The postwar period was one of corruption and injustice.

A MODERN STATE

In 1893 another political "boss"—though a far less corrupt one than Mahone—assumed a prominence that would last for twenty-six years. Thomas S. Martin was elected by the General Assembly to the United States Senate in that year. He held this post until his death in 1919.

Beginning in the 1890s semblances of the old prosperity began to appear in scattered areas of the state. In 1894 the boundary line between Maryland and Virginia on the Delmarva Peninsula was settled. It had been disputed for more than two hundred years. Another boundary, that with North Carolina and Tennessee, had been in question for more than a hundred years when it was settled in 1903 by the United States Supreme Court.

In 1901 a convention met to write a new constitution. This was never approved by the voters, but in 1902 was "proclaimed" at the convention and "approved" by the legislature. Although it improved the old constitution in many ways, it provided means by which poor and illiterate voters—both white and black but especially black—were kept from voting.

In 1907 an exposition was held at Hampton Roads to commemorate the three-hundredth anniversary of the founding of Jamestown. The Atlantic Squadron of the United States Navy, as well as ships from Europe and Japan, were anchored in the harbor during the exposition as a part of the many attractions. However, partly because the location was hard to reach, attendance was low and the exposition lost money. Ten years later part of the Norfolk Naval Base would be built on the site of the exposition.

In Staunton a government change came in 1908 that had far-reaching effects. The city hired a professional administrator, called a city manager, to operate the day-to-day business of the city. The mayor and city council passed laws and made policy, but the city manager was responsible for carrying them out. Staunton was the first city ever to use the city manager plan, and it has been copied by many cities all over the world.

Virginia-born Thomas Woodrow Wilson was inaugurated as President of the United States in 1913. His administration was dominated by World War I. During the war, prosperity returned to Virginia, with wartime industries and great military establishments in the commonwealth. The port and naval base at Hampton Roads sent thousands of tons of goods to foreign and domestic ports. Nearly 300,000 soldiers sailed to Europe from there. The Newport News Shipbuilding and Dry Dock Company built 20 percent of all the tonnage of the United States Navy in World War I.

Fifty thousand troops were trained at Camp Lee, one of the largest military camps in the country. Camp Stuart, where troops were shipped out, Camp Humphrey, where engineers were trained, and Langley Field, one of the country's main aviation centers, were other busy military centers. In this war 91,623 people from Virginia were in the armed services, and 1,635 lost their lives. The worldwide influenza epidemic of 1918 claimed 11,641 more lives in Virginia.

The state government was entirely reorganized in 1927, when Harry Flood Byrd was governor, to simplify and improve government service to the people. Many new industries also came to

Virginia in the late 1920s. It was also during Byrd's tenure as governor that segregation of black and white people became law, rather than a custom that had begun when slaves were freed after the Civil War. Byrd went on to the United States Senate and to a position of dominance over Virginia's politics that lasted until the mid-1960s.

THE DEPRESSION

The Great Depression of the 1930s did not affect Virginia as seriously as it did the other southern states. This is partly because the state had a better balance of farming, industry, and trade. Many more farmers had modern equipment, too. A serious drought in 1930, however, made conditions worse. In 1932 tobacco sold at such a low price that many Virginia growers could not continue to work. A similar situation occurred in the state's coal mines. Many city dwellers returned to family farms because they could more easily find food and housing there.

Shenandoah National Park, first conceived in the 1890s, was officially established in 1935. It is one of the nation's most popular national parks, and includes the beautiful Skyline Drive. At about this same time The Virginia Museum of Fine Arts was founded. It was the first state art museum.

Because so many actors were unemployed during the Depression of the 1930s, and because so few people had money, a man named Robert Porterfield decided to make these two facts work for each other. He founded the Barter Theater, where the admission price was food or another commodity other than cash.

THE SECOND WORLD WAR AND AFTER

During World War II, 214,903 Virginia men and women saw service. The Newport News Shipyard built 185 ships for wartime use. The population of the Hampton Roads area grew so fast that homes, schools, and food were in short supply for the

38

newcomers. During the war racial problems continued and in some ways increased. In 1943 the Richmond *Times-Dispatch* became the first southern newspaper to suggest that public transportation be integrated. It would not be until the mid-1950s that this integration would take place.

The state's mental hospitals were greatly improved in the mid-1950s. Twenty million additional dollars were spent on them, and they were able to add four thousand new beds plus a thousand new employees. Food service was improved and there was more money available for day-to-day expenditures.

In 1954 the United States Supreme Court handed down a historic decision outlawing school segregation. Until then Virginia had operated under a policy of "separate but equal" schools for black and white children. Schools in three localities were closed rather than integrated. But on February 2, 1959, formerly all-white schools in Norfolk and Arlington received their first black students. In that same year enabling legislation for integrating all state schools was put through the General Assembly.

The 1960s brought great prosperity to Virginia. The state attracted much new industry, added many vocational and technical schools, and made significant improvements at the Hampton Roads ports.

Virginia's third state constitution was approved in 1970, replacing the 1902 document. Pressure had come for a constitutional revision when it became obvious that the old constitution was too long and had become obsolete. The new constitution allowed the state more borrowing privileges so it could provide services to more people.

The state also has become much more urbanized since the late 1950s. The cities near Washington, D.C., Fredericksburg, Richmond, and the cities on both sides of the Hampton Roads harbor have grown rapidly in population. Some writers estimate that today three-fifths of the state's population live in this urban corridor.

The first Republican governor since 1886 went into office in 1970. He was A. Linwood Holton, who defeated William Battle in a close race. In 1972 Harry F. Byrd, Jr., followed in his father's footsteps by entering the United States Senate. The Republican Party also won more congressional seats in the 1972 election than it had since 1886.

Several Virginia families claim to be descended from Pocohontas (right) and her husband, John Rolfe. Their son, Thomas, who settled in Virginia after growing up in London, married Jane Poythress, and they had a large number of descendants. Painting by R.M. Sully.

The late 1970s saw much concern in the state over the crippling of the seafood industry, caused principally by the release of an insecticide called Kepone into the waters of the James River. Traces of this poisonous substance were found in fish as far away as Chesapeake Bay.

THE PEOPLE OF THE OLD DOMINION

The founders of Virginia were English, but it was not long before people from other European countries began to come to the Old Dominion. After 1685 French refugees became the largest non-English European group. Large numbers of German and Scottish people settled in the mountain regions, and many of their descendants still live there. While there are in Virginia today people with backgrounds of almost every country, the commonwealth has never been the "melting pot" that some other states were.

The Church of England was the established church of early Virginia. On many occasions those who professed other faiths were persecuted or driven away. However, within the first century and a half of European settlement, people who had other beliefs were tolerated. Virginia's first Jewish congregation was established in 1789.

The people who lived in Virginia's mountains were isolated for centuries from the culture and way of life of the coastal lands. But as television, fast transportation, and better education reach into the most remote areas, this isolation is gradually dying out.

Natural Treasures

ON THE LAND

In spite of more than three hundred years of use, the forests of Virginia still cover over 60 percent of the commonwealth's land area. Land that is not usable for anything else is being restored to forest at the rate of about 100,000 acres (about 40,000 hectares) per year. Although the vast reaches of pine forest are growing smaller, the land area of hardwoods is increasing. The George Washington and the Jefferson National Forests were created to conserve and promote the best uses of the forest resources.

The Galax-Hillsville area is said to have the largest variety of plant life in the United States. Galax is named for a distinctive and handsome mountain evergreen plant of the same name. Across the state are the lotus gardens of Virginia Beach. They are the last large stands of American lotus in the nation.

Many kinds of wildlife found by the original European settlers have disappeared—among them buffalo, wolves, and panthers—but a variety of animals and birds still can be found. Perhaps the most interesting of these are the wild ponies of Chincoteague and Assateague Islands. These are not true ponies but a kind of stunted horse.

Wild ponies graze in the salt marsh of Assateague Island.

Tangier Island, in Chesapeake Bay. The bay area is noted for its excellent crabs oysters, and clams.

IN THE EARTH

Virginia has notable deposits of coal, zinc, titanium, limestone, soapstone, slate, clay, gypsum, and lead. Coal is most prominent in the southwestern part of the state, where coal mining is an important industry. Most of the state's minerals are found away from the Piedmont and Tidewater regions of the eastern part of the state. Titanium is especially predominant in the Blue Ridge Mountains of central Virginia. A strain of gold-bearing rock runs through the central Piedmont area.

Other minerals found in Virginia include sandstone, black marble, shale, dolomite, greenstone, feldspar, mica, marl, granite, barite, glass sand, salt, cyanide, iron, manganese, graphite, pyrrhotite, and pyrite. Some of the more unusual minerals are found there, too, such as aplite, ilmenite, rutile, and kyanite.

THE WATERS

The Cheapeake Bay area is noted for its crabs, oysters, and clams. These are served in fine restaurants of the area, and "crabbing" and "clamming" are favorite "outdoor sports" for residents and visitors alike. In the ocean off the coast of Accomack and Northampton countries, on the Delmarva Peninsula, are found menhaden. This herringlike fish lives in coastal Atlantic waters and is used for oil, fertilizer, or bait.

People Use Their Treasures

MOTHER OF MANUFACTURING

Manufacturing in the United States was begun in Virginia in 1608 by the Jamestown colonists, who built a glass factory. Visitors to Jamestown today can see that first primitive factory reproduced. Knicker-clad workers puff out their cheeks to blow the glass just as it was done in the early days.

America's first iron furnace was set up in 1619 by John Berkeley near present Chesterfield. Richard Dawson of Gloucester County was the first person in America to "make money" when he struck the country's first coins.

There were many water-powered grain and saw mills in early times. George Washington proudly claimed that the flour made in his mill was "equal in quality to any made in this country."

Today the value of Virginia manufacturing is about seven billion dollars a year. The chemical and textile industries are the largest employers in the commonwealth. Virginia ranks first among all the states in the production of synthetic fibers, turning out a mammoth 25 percent of all such materials produced in the country.

Manufacturing started early in Virginia at such places as Mt. Vernon, where Washington had his own flour mill. Mabry Mill (below) was built in 1910.

Wood products alone in Virginia are worth over a billion dollars a year. John David Bassett created the world's largest wood furniture producing empire, with headquarters at Bassett, Virginia. This one company turns out a large percentage of all the wood furniture made in the United States. Wood milling remains one of the state's important industries.

The largest single manufacturing firm in the state is the gigantic Newport News Shipbuilding and Dry Dock Company. This has long been one of the most unusual firms. Its founder, famed industrialist Collis Potter Huntington, poured more than ten million dollars into the shipyard before his death in 1900 without ever realizing a cent of income from its operation. He was content to say: "We build good ships here at a profit if we can, at a loss if we must, but always good ships."

Those "good ships" have included the mammoth aircraft super-carrier *Enterprise,* the first nuclear-powered carrier and the largest ship in the world, and the passenger liner *United States,* holder of the record for the fastest transatlantic crossing. Many nuclear-powered submarines have also slid into the waters from the Newport News ways.

Babcock and Wilcox of Lynchburg is the world's leading producer of steam-generating equipment. They have now also become experts in the highly specialized skill of producing commercial-type atomic power plants. One of their accomplishments in this field was the power plant for the first United States nuclear cargo ship, *Savannah.*

Another Virginia company ranks as one of the three largest processors of frozen foods in the United States. This is the Morton company of Crozet. A small but interesting part of the food industry is the Smithfield ham business. More than 350 years ago the Indians taught the colonists how to cure the hams from razorback hogs, using hickory smoke. Today Smithfield is known as the "hickory smoking capital of the world."

Virginia's ten thousand fishermen have a catch valued at many millions of dollars a year. The James River became especially famous for its oystering, producing a plump bivalve that is one of the most delicious found anywhere.

Birthplace of Cyrus McCormick, Steele's Tavern, Virginia. The world's first mechanical harvester originated in the shop at the right.

SEEKING AND FINDING

Virginia is a leader among the southern states in scientific research. One of the major developments in this field was the Space Radiation Effects Laboratory which went into operation near Newport News in 1966 as a project of the National Aeronautics and Space Administration. The Space Radiation Effects Laboratory is a part of a unique scientific agency known as the Virginia Associated Research Center, operated jointly by the College of William and Mary, the University of Virginia, and Virginia Polytechnic Institute.

The Atlantic Research Corporation, founded in 1949 by Dr. Arthur Sloan and Dr. Arch Scurlock, is located about five miles (eight kilometers) south of the District of Columbia. One of its principal projects has been the development of solid fuels for rockets.

Searching for new facts and ideas is in the Virginia tradition. One of the most far-reaching inventions in the world's history was developed in the Old Dominion. Working on his farm, Walnut Grove, near Greenville, Cyrus Hall McCormick in 1831 perfected a machine that would cut and gather grain mechanically. At that time he was only twenty-two years old. Sixteen years later he had sold only 778 reapers, so he moved west to be nearer the grain country.

45

At Raphine Hall, near Walnut Grove, James Ethan Allen Gibbs is credited with inventing in 1857 a particular kind of sewing machine—the "twisted loop rotary hook" type.

AGRICULTURE

Today's agriculture owes much to the foundation laid by generations of Virginia farmers large and small. The total agricultural income of Virginia is well over a billion dollars annually. Livestock and crops are almost equally balanced in providing farm income.

Tobacco brings in almost a third of the Virginia farmer's crop money. When John Rolfe began the country's first experiment in tobacco raising, he was quite satisfied with his efforts and described his tobacco as "strong, sweet and pleasant as any under the sun." Danville is one of the most famous centers of tobacco growing in the South, noted for its bright leaf, and the Danville and South Boston tobacco auctions rank among the most important.

There is great variety in Virginia's agriculture. The truck farms of the Eastern Shore produce fresh vegetables and small fruits on a large scale; inland from Norfolk, peanuts, soybeans, and hogs are the major items. Far northern Virginia is one of the nation's most important apple-growing regions. In Frederick County alone more than seven-hundred thousand apple trees blanket the countryside with pink and white blooms in the spring. The Albemarle pippin apple was said to have been a favorite of Queen Victoria, who often sent for supplies of them to be delivered to the palace.

In many counties of Virginia there has been a changeover from field crops to dairy and beef cattle. Broiler chickens are also important income producers.

Cotton was once a principal Virginia crop. At one time many people held great hope for the silk industry, and mulberry trees and silkworms were brought in very early. Virginia silkworms spun three hundred pounds (136 kilograms) of silk which Governor William Berkeley proudly sent to King Charles II in 1660 for the royal coronation robes. But the silk industry did not succeed in Virginia.

46

MINING AND MINERALS

The annual value of mineral production in Virginia exceeds a billion dollars. The first commercial coal-mining operation in the United States began in Virginia in 1750. Today coal is the leading mineral industry of the state, and Virginia is sixth in coal among all the states.

Stone quarried in Virginia is second in value of the state's minerals. Sand and gravel rank third and zinc is the leading metallic mineral. Lead has long been important, even before the Fort Chiswell lead mines supplied bullets for the Revolutionary War.

TRANSPORTATION AND COMMUNICATION

When the automobile first became popular, Virginia's roads and highways were notoriously bad. But over the next fifty years the situation was completely reversed. Today Virginia's state roads and highways total over 50,000 miles (over 80,000 kilometers). The commonwealth ranks third among all the states in total miles (total kilometers) of state-administered roads and streets. The great interstate road system in Virginia provides 1,056 miles (about 1,700 kilometers) of superhighways.

Virginia's first railroad, the Chesterfield Railroad, began operating in 1831. Its cars were drawn by horses and it carried coal over the thirteen miles (twenty-one kilometers) from the mines to Richmond. Each car held only fifty-six bushels (about twenty hectoliters) of coal. In 1836 the Richmond, Fredericksburg and Potomac Railroad first carried frightened passengers across the state at the breathtaking speed of ten miles (sixteen kilometers) per hour!

Today Virginia has about four thousand miles (about sixty-five hundred kilometers) of railroad tracks. Included in these are part of the lines of the Norfolk and Western Railway, with headquarters in Virginia.

One of the world's most spectacular highways links Virginia's eastern peninsula with the rest of the Old Dominion by road for the first time in history. This is the Cheapeake Bay Bridge-Tunnel. To build this twenty-three mile-long (thirty-seven kilometers) marvel, engineers constructed four artificial "islands" in the middle of the bay. These islands anchored the ends of the bridges and provided entrances for two tunnels which burrow beneath the bay. The tunnels left two wide channels in the bay for the passage of ships. With this construction, no disaster could close vital Hampton Roads to naval ships.

The Norfolk-Hampton Roads area has been under the influence of seagoing commerce ever since the first merchants dropped anchor there nearly three hundred years ago. Commercial steamboats began operation to Virginia ports in 1813. The Hampton Roads shipping center includes Newport News, Portsmouth, and Chesapeake, in addition to Norfolk. Among other distinctions, Hampton Roads leads all other United States ports in coal dumping and is the leading Atlantic coast port in the export of grain. More than five thousand ships a year call at Hampton Roads.

The country's first canal was opened in 1790, running parallel with the James River for seven miles (just over eleven kilometers) to connect Richmond with Westham. The James River Canal Company, which built this canal, was sponsored by George Washington, John Marshall, Edmund Randolph, and other prominent citizens. The old Potomac Canal, also sponsored by Washington, was a forerunner of the later Chesapeake and Ohio Canal. In 1812 a canal cutting through the Dismal Swamp linked the waters of Chesapeake Bay and Albemarle Sound.

Vast Dulles International Airport at Chantilly, with its pagoda-shaped control tower and swooping main building, heads the list of Virginia's seventy-six airports. Dulles is one of the world's largest air fields.

Virginia possesses one of the true distinctions in the newspaper field. The Alexandria *Gazette* is the nation's oldest continuously operating daily paper. It is the continuation of the Virginia *Journal* and Alexandria *Advertiser,* started in 1784. The Virginia *Gazette* of Williamsburg, a weekly, was the first newspaper to be published in the commonwealth.

Human Treasures

PROUD PRESIDENTIAL PARENT

Eight American Presidents were born in Virginia. Ohio, which also is known as the "mother of Presidents," claims eight Presidents, too, but one is William Henry Harrison, who was born in Virginia. However, it must be added that some of the Virginia-born Presidents spent much of their lives and gained their fame outside the state.

Four of the first five—George Washington, Thomas Jefferson, James Madison, and James Monroe—are know as the "Virginia Dynasty" because they are all from Virginia.

HIS COUNTRY'S FATHER

Although George Washington has been given much fame as the "father of his country," few people today recognize that he was a lively and vital person of keen wit and unusual humor, with a wide capacity for understanding.

After Jane Butler Washington, first wife of Augustine Washington, died, Augustine married Mary Ball of Sandy Point. Their first child was born February 22, 1732, and named George. When George was sixteen he went to live with his half-brother Lawrence, who had built a house called Mount Vernon on the Hunting Creek plantation. Hunting Creek was built in 1669 by the family's first settlers in America.

Lawrence planned to enlist George in the British navy, but when Mary Ball Washington heard of this she promptly brought her son back to the Ferry Farm near Fredericksburg. Her husband had settled his family there several years before his death. The history of the world might have been much different if George Washington had become a British naval officer!

In 1748 the powerful Lord Fairfax hired youthful George Washington to survey his enormous estate. Washington set out, admiring

George Washington in consultation with Thomas Jefferson and Alexander Hamilton, *by Constantino Brumidi.*

the scenery as he passed "through most beautiful groves of Sugar Trees and spent ye best part of ye Day in admiring ye Trees and richness of ye Land." Such things always interested Washington; his great ambition was to become the foremost agriculturist in America. His many later experiments in advanced farming (including the then little-known method of crop rotation) and livestock methods might have qualified him for that title. On the lighter side, he once won a prize for "raising the largest jackass." However, much more significant prizes would be in store for him.

Demonstrating his exceptional military and organizational abilities in the Indian wars, Washington next added to his political know-how as a member of the House of Burgesses. The House passed resolutions to thank Washington for his service in the Indian wars, but when he rose to speak he was too embarrassed to find the words. John Robinson, the Speaker of the House, said, "Sit down, Mr. Washington. Your modesty surpasses your valor, and that is beyond any language at my command."

In the Revolution it is probable that no other man in the United States could have kept together the disorganized, poorly trained, often starving, military forces of the newborn country. Time and again only the calm persuasion of the commander-in-chief and his eloquent pleas for money and food and other support kept the Revolution going.

50

When Washington was president of the Constitutional Convention, that same calm manner soothed many controversies and paved the way for a strong government. We still have this legacy of the convention's work. Would the new country's government have been able to endure the turmoil and disagreements, the bitter battles among those who disagreed with it, if it had not been for Washington's judgment and vast experience during his two terms as President? Many authorities believe it would not.

The complications of putting into operation a form of government completely new in world history in a poverty stricken, war-ravaged, disorganized country composed of separate states jealous of their rights was almost beyond imagination. Yet when Washington had served two terms and refused a third, he was able to pass on to John Adams a government that was running quite smoothly and with great promise of things to come. Washington was the only President ever to receive the unanimous vote of the Electoral College.

In 1797 Washington returned to Mount Vernon, which he had inherited from Lawrence, his half-brother. There he planned to work on his beloved agriculture. Possibly he had hopes of fulfilling his long-time ambition to learn to play the flute and to enjoy other pleasures that his life of service for his country had never permitted.

In 1752 Washington had proposed to Miss Elizabeth Fauntleroy, but she had coolly turned him down because of the smallpox marks on his face. He had written a touching letter to her father, saying, "I propose . . . to wait on Miss Betsy, in hopes of a revocation of the former cruel sentence and see if I can meet with any alteration in my favor." But this was not to be.

When he married Martha Custis, his bride, a widow, had two children. Martha Parke Custis died in her teens without marrying. John Parke Custis lived until just after the Revolutionary War and left a widow and four children. Both the Washingtons were terribly grieved, and at John's deathbed Washington said to John's wife Eleanor, "I adopt the two youngest children as my own."

These children were Eleanor Parke Custis and George Washington Parke Custis, who were raised at Mount Vernon. Both were very much cherished, especially Washington's beloved Nelly Custis.

Washington was to have only two quiet years at home after his presidency. On one of his regular trips to his mill he caught a cold, and died on December 14, 1799.

"MR. JEFFERSON"

If Thomas Jefferson had not won even greater fame in other fields, he would certainly still have great renown as one of this country's leading architects. He would be recognized as a leading writer and his achievements in education place him in the rank of leading educators. Given more time he probably would have become an outstanding inventor. Like Benjamin Franklin, Jefferson was one of the most versatile of all widely-known Americans.

Thomas Jefferson was born on April 13, 1743, at Shadwell, the farm of his father, Peter Jefferson. It was not far from where the son later built his own estate, Monticello. He was educated at William and Mary College and gained his first political experience in the House of Burgesses.

Possibly his greatest fame came at the age of thirty-three when he drafted the ringing phrases of the Declaration of Independence and established his reputation as a great social and political philosopher. As governor of Virginia following Patrick Henry, he was not especially distinguished. Later, he became minister (ambassador) to France, following Benjamin Franklin. There he saw the horrors of the beginning of the French Revolution.

Jefferson served as Washington's Secretary of State, then as Vice-President and then as President, winning the post from Aaron Burr through only one vote—that of Alexander Hamilton. (Burr would later kill Hamilton in a very famous duel at Weehawken, New Jersey.) As President, the highlights of Jefferson's terms were the successful war with the pirates who plied the Mediterranean Sea, the magnificent purchase of the vast Louisiana Territory—which stretched far beyond the Mississippi River—and the exploration of that territory by Meriwether Lewis and William Clark, both also Virginia natives.

*Left: Portrait of
Thomas Jefferson
by Thomas Sully.
Below: Jefferson's
home, Monticello,
In Charlottesville.*

After his second term as President, Jefferson retired, becoming known as "the Sage of Monticello." He had barely begun Monticello, near Charlottesville, when he brought his bride there on horseback through a January blizzard in 1772. The handsome, ingeniously planned house was not finished until 1809. He loved "gadgets" and built dozens of labor-saving devices and curiosities of his own design into his home, such as disappearing beds, dumbwaiters, unique ventilating and lighting systems, unusual clocks, and many other items.

His fame was so great that many people, sometimes as many as forty or fifty in a day, visited him at Monticello. He is still known in Charlottesville simply as "Mr. Jefferson." He was so hospitable and generous to the many visitors that he had very much reduced his financial circumstances by the time he died in 1826. His widow was left with comparatively little property. Strangely, the writer of the Declaration of Independence died on the Fourth of July exactly fifty years after the Declaration had been first proclaimed.

His epitaph, which Jefferson wrote for himself, reads simply: "Here was buried Thomas Jefferson, author of the Declaration of American Independence, of the statute of Virginia for religious freedom and father of the University of Virginia."

He made no mention of the Presidency or his accomplishments in many fields such as architecture. The French Marquis de Chastellux as early as 1782 wrote: "We may safely aver that Mr. Jefferson is the first American who has consulted the fine arts to know how he should shelter himself from the weather." In addition to Monticello, Jefferson's greatest architectural monuments are the early buildings of the University of Virginia and the state capitol. Many of the fine old houses of Virginia were either designed by Jefferson or built following his suggestions.

VIRGINIA'S OTHER CHIEFS

The greatest work of James Madison, born at Port Conway on March 16, 1751, lives on today in the Constitution of the United

Painting of James Madison by Edgar Parker.

States. His work in drafting the Constitution was so significant that he has become known as the "Father of the Constitution." After the Constitution was operating, Madison introduced the Bill of Rights so that the freedoms implied under the Constitution would be more surely guaranteed.

He served as Secretary of State under Jefferson and became President in 1808. He lost popularity because of his poor handling of the War of 1812, nicknamed "Mr. Madison's War." After his second term, he retired to his estate, Montpelier.

In 1794 Madison married the beautiful widow Dolley Payne. In Washington at the White House and at Montpelier she gained the reputation as one of the most popular and talented hostesses in the history of the country. James Madison died June 28, 1836.

James Monroe fought in the Revolution and later served as United States Senator, minister to France, and governor of Virginia. Later he returned to France where he carried out Jefferson's instructions and brilliantly negotiated the purchase of the Louisiana Territory from Napoleon. Under James Madison, he served as Secretary of State, then as Secretary of War.

Monroe was elected President in 1816. During his terms he solved the problem of the border with Canada and made it possible for the long Canadian border to be undefended—one of the true moves toward peace of all time. He also managed to settle the border dispute between the United States and Russia in the northwest. Florida finally became a part of the United States during his term, completing a project Monroe had not been able to finish when he bought Louisiana for Jefferson.

The best known of his accomplishments came about when he decided, in consultation with his friend and mentor Thomas Jefferson, to try to stop the interference of European governments in the affairs of countries in the Western Hemisphere. He proclaimed a policy that the United States would protect its neighbors. This policy has come to be known as the Monroe Doctrine. Its effects have been among the most far-reaching in the whole history of international relations.

Monroe was born in Westmoreland County on April 28, 1758. He died in New York City on the Fourth of July, 1831, five years to the day after Jefferson died.

William Henry Harrison was born at Berkeley in Charles City County on February 9, 1773. He was a son of Benjamin Harrison, who was a signer of the Declaration of Independence and one of a long dynasty of Harrisons. William Henry Harrison gained most of his fame as governor of the Northwest Territory and as a general in the Indian wars. His victory at the Battle of Tippecanoe in Indiana provided his campaign slogan, "Tippecanoe and Tyler, Too." But after his inauguration as the ninth President he served only thirty-one days before he died. He never recovered from a cold he caught during his inaugural ceremonies.

Harrison's Vice-President was also a Virginian. John Tyler was born March 29, 1790, at Greenway Estate, also in Charles City County and very close to Harrison's birthplace. He was graduated from William and Mary College, served in the Virginia legislature, as the state's governor, and finally as United States Senator. In 1840 he was elected Vice-President and took over the Presidency on the death of Harrison. This first death of a President in office was a significant moment, because there was some question until this time as to whether the Vice-President had the right to succeed or whether a new President would be elected. By taking over the office, Tyler decided the question. One of the high points of his term as President was the addition of the Republic of Texas as a state. He failed to win nomination for a full term.

Tyler was opposed to secession and tried to keep peace at Fort Sumter. However, when the Civil War came he supported the South. He died January 18, 1862, before he could take his elected place in the Confederate Congress.

On November 24, 1784, Zachary Taylor was born in Orange County, but his parents moved to Kentucky when he was only nine months old. Forty years of military service came to its high point in his victories in the war with Mexico, where he became known as "Old Rough and Ready." His wartime popularity carried him into office as the twelfth President of the United States, but he had served only sixteen months when he died of typhus fever on July 9, 1850. (Another hero of the Mexican War, Winfield Scott, was also a native of Virginia, born near Petersburg.)

The man who became the twenty-eighth President, Thomas Woodrow Wilson, was born in the manse of the First Presbyterian Church of Staunton on December 28, 1856, while his father was the minister there. Except for the period in which he studied law at the University of Virginia, little of Wilson's adult life was spent in his native state. After making a fine reputation as governor of New Jersey, he won his first election to the Presidency over a divided Republican Party. A campaign based on the slogan "He kept us out of war" brought Wilson his second term, but shortly afterward the United States entered World War I.

In order, as he said, to save the world from future wars, Wilson proposed that a League of Nations be formed. But he could not persuade Congress to permit the United States to join the League. Worn out and bitterly disappointed over this struggle, he suffered a stroke and never recovered. His second wife, Edith Bolling Galt Wilson, kept the President away from most of his advisers and government officials during his long illness, and many felt that she had taken on the job of "unofficial President."

When Warren Harding was inaugurated as President in 1920, Wilson made one of his late, rare public appearances. He died February 3, 1924. One of his highest distinctions was the award of the Nobel Prize for Peace in 1919.

THE LEES

The Lee family was one of the most distinguished in Virginia history. Thomas Lee was the only native Virginian named by the king of England as a royal governor of Virginia. Richard Henry Lee, a leading figure in the Revolution, and Francis Lightfoot Lee were the only two brothers to sign the Declaration of Independence. "Lighthorse Harry" Lee, spectacular Revolutionary War officer and governor of Virginia, was the father of the most famous of all the Lees—Robert Edward Lee.

Robert E. Lee was born at Stratford, the elegant plantation of the Lee family. After graduation from West Point, he had many military

Stratford Hall, Westmoreland County, ancestral home of Robert E. Lee.

assignments, including command of the troops that captured John Brown at Harpers Ferry. Abraham Lincoln offered him command of Union troops, but he felt he could not accept and make war on his own people, although he strongly opposed slavery. He once said, ". . . slavery as an institution is a moral and political evil in any country . . . a greater evil to the white than to the black race."

His spectacular triumphs early in the war helped to maintain a strong South, but not even his military genius could overcome the gradual weakening of the Southern forces. When the war was over, he accepted the presidency of Washington College, which later was renamed Washington and Lee in his honor.

Today this cultured, gentle man of dignity is respected and honored in both North and South for his fine qualities.

There are many other remarkable Virginia natives with public careers. Peyton Randolph was the first president of the First Continental Congress. William Fleming was the only person from west of the Blue Ridge to sit in the Continental Congress. Sam Houston, the only man ever to be governor of two states, president of a republic, and United States Senator, was a Virginian. In the health field there was Walter Reed, discoverer of the cause of yellow fever. One of America's great military strategists, Thomas Jonathan (Stonewall) Jackson, was from Virginia, as was George Mason, the aristocrat who wrote the bill of rights in the Virginia constitution, a model for that of the United States Constituion. Virginia also gave us Robert "King" Carter, whose descendants number eight governors of Virginia, three signers of the Declaration of Independence, two Presidents, a chief justice, a bishop, and General Robert E. Lee. John Marshall, often listed as our greatest chief justice, and George C. Marshall, architect of the United States World War II policies and originator of the Marshall Plan to aid war-torn Europe, are two more members of the state's famous legacy.

Three of Virginia's Civil War heroes were women. Molly Tynes made a forty-mile (sixty-four-kilometer) Paul Revere-type ride across the countryside to warn of a coming Union attack. On the other side was Elizabeth Van Lew, who risked her life at Richmond as a Union agent. Outstanding among war heroines was Sally

Tompkins, head of a Confederate hospital, who was raised to the rank of captain in the Confederate army.

One of the best-known women of her time was Nancy Langhorne, born in Danville. She married Viscount Waldorf Astor, and as Lady Astor became a powerful British politician, the first woman ever to sit in the British Parliament.

POLITICAL POWERS

For twenty-six years, from his first election to the United States Senate in 1893 to his death in 1919, Thomas S. Martin dominated Virginia's political scene. He was an astute politician and he built up a strong organization of loyal supporters.

Efforts were made from time to time to break the power of Martin's organization. Martin himself was always loyal to the Democratic party and promoted its programs even when he did not entirely agree with them. But he apparently took no personal advantage from his position, and died a poor man. His main pleasure seemed to be in having and wielding power.

It was not long after Martin died that another, more powerful man would come into prominence in Virginia. Born in 1886, Harry Flood Byrd became a state senator at age twenty-eight, in 1916. In 1923 he was victorious in a roadbuilding bond issue referendum. This victory was the start of his prominence and influence. In 1926 Byrd became governor of Virginia and acknowledged leader of the state's Democratic party.

In 1932 Byrd was appointed to the United States Senate, and he supported Franklin Delano Roosevelt's policies until 1933. After that, and for the rest of his career, he was nationally known for his ultraconservative positions on most issues within Virginia and in Congress.

Byrd's political machine controlled Virginia politics from the 1920s into the 1960s. Old and in poor health, Byrd retired from the Senate in November of 1965 and died in October of 1966. He had been a senator for thirty-two years.

Pocahontas Interposing
for Captain John Smith,
by Charles DeWolf Brownell.

THE PRINCESS AND THE CAPTAIN

Two of the most interesting characters of American history are Captain John Smith and the Indian princess Pocahontas. The survival of the first English colony in America was due mostly to the courage, daring, and experience of Smith. However, he treated the Indians so harshly that he was probably also responsible for many of the later Indian troubles. In his explorations he ranged over much of the coast. He wrote two extraordinary accounts of his explorations:

Pocahontas, supposed to have saved Smith's life, was very much in love with the captain, but he failed to acknowledge this. Several years after Smith went back to England Pocahontas was brought to Jamestown as a captive. She was told that Smith was dead. Before marrying John Rolfe, she was baptized as a Christian and renamed Rebecca. Rolfe took his Indian wife with him to London in 1617, and there she saw Smith.

Although Pocahontas died in London, her son Thomas returned to Virginia after he grew to manhood in London. He came back to the estate given to his father as a dowry by Emperor Powhatan—the same estate where John Rolfe introduced tobacco growing. Thomas Rolfe married Jane Poythress, and they had a large number of descendants. The second wife of Woodrow Wilson, Edith Bolling Galt Wilson, was a descendant of Pocahontas through this family.

CREATIVE VIRGINIANS

Many famous characters in literature have been "born" in Virginia. The velvet-suited, white-collared hero *Little Lord Fauntleroy* was created by Frances Hodgson Burnett, who said she based him on the son of a friend in Norfolk. A well-loved song character, Sweet Alice, was created by English writer Thomas Dunn while he was a guest in the Peery house near Tazewell. The song became "Do You Remember Sweet Alice, Ben Bolt?"

Another poet from abroad, Irish Tom Moore, visited Richmond in 1803. His works *The Lake of the Dismal Swamp* and *To the Firefly* were written on this visit.

The orphaned Edgar Allan Poe was adopted by the Allan family of Richmond. He was educated in Richmond and at the University of Virginia. He later said, "I am a Virginian; at least I call myself one." Other Virginia poets were Father Abraham Joseph Ryan, sometimes known as the poet laureate of the South, and John Banister Tabb, another popular Southern poet. Virginia poet George Dillon won the Pulitzer Prize for poetry in 1932.

William Cabell Bruce was awarded the Pulitzer Prize for biography in 1918 with his work on Benjamin Franklin.

Willa Cather, born in Winchester; Ellen Glasgow; John Warwick Daniel, author of the *Lame Lion of Lynchburg;* Mary Johnston; Francis Parkinson Keyes, born at Charlottesville; and James Branch Cabell are other well-known Virginia writers.

Three prominent entertainers were born in Virginia. Singer Kate Smith is a native of Greenville. Francis Xavier Bushman, one of the first great movie stars, who appeared in 402 films, was born in Norfolk. Famed and much-loved entertainer Bill "Bojangles" Robinson was born in Richmond.

FORMER SLAVES AND THEIR DESCENDANTS

On a list of the household "goods" owned by planter Jones Burroughs is a notation, "One Negro boy, 'Booker,' value $400.00."

That little boy grew up and became Booker T. Washington, one of America's greatest educators.

He had been given his name Booker because he had loved books almost from his earliest days. After emancipation he went with his mother to West Virginia, where he worked in a salt furnace and also a coal mine. He kept up his schoolwork and later was graduated from Hampton Institute, where he worked as a janitor to earn his board. He then taught and studied at Wayland Seminary in Washington, D. C. His success in a faculty position at Hampton Institute led to his being asked to organize the Normal and Industrial Institute for Negroes (now Tuskegee Institute) at Tuskegee, Alabama. His work at Tuskegee has ranked him as one of the leading American educators of all time. Washington's autobiography, *Up from Slavery,* is one of the best known of all such works.

When the Richmond Theater burned in 1811, a heroic slave, Gilbert Hunt, saved twenty women and children by catching them in his arms as they were thrown from upper windows to escape the flames. A devoted gravedigger, remembered only as "Yellow Fever Jack," was the hero of the Norfolk yellow fever epidemic of 1855.

Other prominent Virginia blacks include Dr. James H. Solomon Russell, born a slave, who founded St. Paul's Normal and Industrial School at Lawrenceville. Reverend James H. Holmes's First African Baptist Church has five thousand members. Dr. Daniel Norton, Robert Norton, James Bland, and Dr. Thomas Bayne were important leaders after the emancipation. Of Dr. Bayne, a dentist, it was said that he was "one of the shrewdest politicians of his day, whose ready tongue enabled him easily to turn aside the ridicule that met any Negro representative who rose to speak."

REVOLUTIONARY HEROES

Virginia heroes of the Revolutionary War were many. General John Cropper singlehandedly drove off an entire British raiding party near Accomac. Peter Francisco fought an entire brigade by himself and was known as "Virginia's Hercules."

63

The Reverend John Muhlenburg supported the Revolution enthusiastically. In 1774 he drafted a freedom resolution, and in January 1776 he preached a sermon on the text: "There is a time to every purpose . . . a time to war, and a time to peace." At the height of his dramatic address, the minister threw off his robes and displayed the uniform of a colonel in the Revolutionary army.

Another little-known but valiant patriot was Colonel Richard W. R.F. Lewis, brother-in-law of George Washington. Colonel Lewis completely outfitted three entire regiments of troops wholly at his own expense. He even presented a ship to the "Virginia Navy." His contributions to the cause were so great that he died in debt.

Other unusual Virginians include John Lynch, the Quaker who founded Lynchburg when he was only seventeen years old. His brother Charles Lynch gave such harsh treatment to Tories (British loyalists) and criminals during the Revolution that his name was given to the term *Lynch law,* which means to hang an alleged criminal without a trial. Totopotomoi, chief of the Pamunkey Indians, gave his life fighting to defend the colonists against the English. "Mad" Ann Bailey avenged the killing of her husband by Indians with a long career as scout, spy, messenger, and Indian hunter.

Patrick Henry, born in Hanover County on May 29,1736, gained early fame as an orator while he practiced law. His voice was so strong it was said he could give orders to his slaves half a mile (.8 kilometer) away. His remarkable personal life included two wives and fifteen children. During his stormy political career his speeches gave the English language some of its best-known quotations.

He served five years as governor of Virginia. One of his greatest accomplishments as governor was authorizing the expedition of George Rogers Clark in present-day Illinois and Indiana (then considered part of Virginia), which won the west for the United States.

He originally opposed the Constitution of the United States, but when George Washington appealed to him, he made a speech at the Charlotte Courthouse for the support of the President and the federal government. This speech, one of his last official acts, was in the best "fiery" oratory of his earlier days. He died on June 6, 1799, just a few months before Washington died.

Teaching and Learning

As early as 1618 the people of Virginia had chartered "the college and university of Virginia" at Henricopolis, making it the first college to be chartered in the present United States. However, after Henricopolis was destroyed in the massacre of 1622, plans for the University of Henrico were laid aside. The idea of a college was revived when in 1693 their majesties William and Mary granted a charter for a college at Williamsburg to bear their names. James Blair, who had gone to England to rouse interest in such a college, came back to Williamsburg bearing the charter, money, and land rights from the crown and from private parties, and a plan by England's greatest architect, Christopher Wren, for the principal building.

In 1694 the college received the only coat of arms ever granted an American college. As payment for its twenty thousand acres (eight thousand hectares) of endowed land, the college is still supposed to pay to the governor each year two copies of Latin verse. Also included in the college's endowment is three hundred pounds sterling donated by several parties. In 1776 America's best-known honorary scholastic society, Phi Beta Kappa, was founded at William and Mary. George Washington was made the school's chancellor in 1788.

Although the College of William and Mary was the second to be founded in the United States (after Harvard University), it has not had continuous operation. It suspended its operations in the wartime years from 1861 to 1865 and was closed from 1881 to 1889. One of America's leading educators, Dr. Lyle Gardiner Tyler, reopened the college in 1889 and served as its president for thirty-one years. In 1906 the College of William and Mary came under state control.

Among the many distinguished persons educated at William and Mary were three Presidents: Jefferson, Monroe, and Tyler. The college established America's first courses in political economy in 1784, and the first school of history in 1803.

Education was one of Thomas Jefferson's greatest interests. As early as 1779 Jefferson had introduced a bill in the Virginia legis-

Above: The lawn and rotunda of the University of Virginia in the spring. Right: These serpentine walls at the University of Virginia were designed by Thomas Jefferson. Below: Statue of Robert E. Lee at Washington and Lee University.

lature to create a university, but it was not until after he retired as President that he was able to get a bill passed (in 1818) to begin a state university. Through Jefferson's persuasion, this was started at Central College, which had been established two years earlier at Charlottesville. University of Virginia classes began in 1825 with forty students and seven faculty members.

The unusual official name of the University was and still is "The Rector and Visitors of the University of Virginia." Jefferson became the first rector and was the guiding genius of the university until his death. He designed its buildings, its serpentine brick walls, and its spacious lawns and "ranges." This was the first institution of higher education in the United States to be separate from church influence.

Jefferson insisted that the narrow curriculum of other American colleges be broadened, and the university was the first to offer music and other more liberal subjects. Students and faculty were given wide freedom; an honor system was established, and students who broke their pledge of honor were dismissed. These freedoms did not extend to women. They were not admitted as students until 1920. However, Mary Washington College was founded in 1908 at Fredericksburg to be the adjunct woman's college of the university. It is still in operations and has some male students.

The University of Virginia has never closed, although only a few students attended between 1861 and 1865 and many of the buildings were used as wartime hospitals. Among the many famous graduates have been Edgar Allan Poe and Woodrow Wilson. Following a rule laid down by Jefferson, the university has never granted an honorary degree.

Washington and Lee University at Lexington was founded as Augusta Academy in 1749 and then known as Liberty Hall. When George Washington donated two hundred shares of James River Canal Company stock, it changed its name to Washington. When Robert E. Lee became its head in 1865, it added his name.

Another famed Lexington institution is Virginia Military Institute, one of the best known of its type in the country. One of its most famous "rats" (the nickname for first-year students) was George Catlett Marshall, later to become General of the Army, Secretary of

Defense, and Secretary of State. Stonewall Jackson was a faculty member, and the institute still proudly remembers the gallant charge of its cadets who tipped the balance of battle at New Market in 1864.

Virginia Polytechnic Institute at Blacksburg is another technical school of great renown. It is often ranked among the top ten engineering schools of the nation. One of its most unusual divisions is the highly regarded Food Processing Laboratory.

Hampton Institute grew out of the desire of former slaves for education, and it expanded rapidly to become one of the most highly regarded institutions of its kind. The tours of its Hampton Singers have added to its worldwide fame.

Among the best-known colleges are Sweet Briar College, Hollins College, and Randolph-Macon College. Randolph-Macon was opened in 1830 and moved to Ashland in 1868. It was the first Methodist Episcopal Church college to be established in the United States. The college for women was established at Lynchburg in 1893. Nobel Prize-winning author Pearl Buck is one of its most distinguished graduates.

Other prominent institutions are the University of Richmond; Virginia Union University, also in Richmond; Old Dominion University, Norfolk, now one of the largest in the state; Virginia Commonwealth University; and Virginia State College, Petersburg.

One of Virginia's early distinguished educators was George Wythe, the first law professor in the United States. He taught John Marshall, Thomas Jefferson, James Monroe, and Henry Clay. His strange death came when he was poisoned by a nephew who was impatient to inherit his uncle's estate.

Virginia lawmakers have shown an interest in education from the beginning. The first discussion in the House of Burgesses was concerned with education. In the will of Benjamin Syms in 1634, two hundred acres (about eighty-one hectares) and eight cows were left to create a school. This became the first free school and the first school with an endowment in all the colonies. The school still operates today as Syms-Eaton Academy at Hampton.

Thomas Jefferson was the first leading figure in favor of free education for all children. It was not until 1870, however, that

Virginia had started on a program of providing such education. In 1905 a popular campaign led to better schools, including high schools as well as colleges for teachers.

Much of Virginia's great improvement in education has come after the close of World War II. Fifty percent of all schools now in use have been built since 1950.

An unusual program of adult education is carried out in the Special Education Program. This provides training at state expense for those who would like to work in particular skilled occupations.

Washington and Lee University, Lexington, Virginia

Enchantment of Virginia

"CARRY ME BACK"

Visitors by the hundreds of thousands hearken to Virginia. Each year tourists spend over a billion dollars in the state.

Almost nowhere else in all the nation is there so much living history—the beginnings of our national traditions at Jamestown, the climax of two great wars, the estates and homes of probably more famous people than anywhere else in the country. All the charm of the older eras blends with the newest and most up-to-date parts of the state.

The sweep of scenery stretches from quiet islands and sunny beaches, past picturesque villages and stirring cities, to the crests of the mountains where the unique Skyline Drive and Blue Ridge Parkway literally carry visitors through the clouds, past postcard vistas of beauty on every side and at every turn.

Virginia pastimes may include deep-sea fishing quickly followed by the wondrous depths of nine spectacular caverns, as well as the attractions of vast national forests and state parks. Even the unexpected fun of skiing in the highlands on artificial snow has been added to Virginia's lure. Innumerable museums, battlefield parks, resident symphony orchestras, and other cultural attractions also may be found. Major theme parks include Busch Gardens and Kings Dominion.

Not the least attractive is the long tradition of good food in Virginia—mouthwatering Virginia hams and delicate spoon bread, deviled crab, plump Virginia oysters on the half shell or roasted and dripping with melted butter, and many other native dishes perfected over the generations.

More and more people are discovering why the state song says "Carry Me Back to Old Virginia."

Opposite: Travelers driving along the Skyline Drive
section of the Blue Ridge Parkway in Virginia have
a magnificent view of the beautiful Blue Ridge Mountains.

VIBRANT PAST, VIBRANT FUTURE

The statues of Stonewall Jackson and other Confederate heroes line Richmond's magnificent Monument Avenue. Statues of those who died fighting face defiantly north; those who returned face the South. Something of the same is true of the city itself; few cities can look to a more inspiring past while facing such an exciting future.

In 1607, the year of Jamestown's founding, an exploring party set up a cross not far from the spot where Richmond's great north-south expressway now strides across the James River on stilts of steel and concrete. In 1644 the spot became a frontier fort. Ninety years later, William Byrd II set aside a tiny part of his vast domain to become a town site, and in 1737, Major William Mayo laid out the first streets and named the new town Richmond.

During the Revolution, Richmond became a target for Tory (British loyalist) raiders led by the American traitor Benedict Arnold. When the state government had to flee the British invaders in 1779, the straggling village suddenly found itself the heir to the capital, long located at aristocratic Williamsburg.

During the Civil War, for four tense and drama-packed years, Richmond stood not only as the capital of Virginia but as the capital of the ill-fated Confederacy. Fortunately, the fires that its own people set to keep it from falling into Northern hands spared much of its historic architecture.

Among the buildings saved was the priceless capitol, designed by Thomas Jefferson. Part of his plan for this classic building was based on the design of the ancient temple built by the Romans at Nîmes, France. It may have been the first modern building to follow the architecture of the ancient masters. Here the New World's oldest continuous legislative assembly still meets; here Aaron Burr was tried for treason; here Virginia approved the Articles of Secession; and here the Confederate Congress held its momentous meetings. The original section of the capitol was finished in 1792. Additions were made in 1904 and 1905.

In the center of the capitol rotunda is the only statue ever created of George Washington from life. Famed sculptor Jean Antoine

The state capitol building in Richmond was designed by Thomas Jefferson.

Houdon followed Washington on his rounds of Mount Vernon until one day Washington began to argue with a salesman about the price of a plow. The gestures of this homespun incident are preserved for posterity in Houdon's remarkable statue.

Also in the capitol is the original plaster model of the capitol building, which Jefferson had made and sent home from France.

Outside is the equestrian statue of Washington by Thomas Crawford, cast in Munich at a cost of $100,000. Also in the capitol complex is the Governor's Mansion built in 1813, and the Virginia State Museum, in the Finance Building.

Few places in American history hold such a thrill as the spot where Patrick Henry thundered forth his call for liberty or death—St. John's Church. Another historic spot is the White House of the Confederacy, wartime home of Jefferson Davis, the President of the Confederation. From the porch Davis's son, Joseph Davis, fell accidentally to his untimely death. Today the building houses what is said to be the largest collection anywhere of Civil War mementos.

Another war memorial is the mighty Memorial Carillon in Byrd Park. It is dedicated to the memory of Virginia's doughboys of World War I. The unique colonnaded marble structure high above the James River has inscribed in it the names of the Virginia men and women who gave their lives in the struggles of later wars.

Richmond's oldest house now is a shrine to Edgar Allan Poe. Other interesting historical homes are the John Marshall House, Virginia House, and Wilton. Famed plantations near the city include Sherwood Forest, home of John Tyler, and Berkeley, birthplace of William Henry Harrison. It is interesting that this mansion was also the birthplace of the familiar wartime bugle call "Taps."

One of the country's most impressive and progressive art museums is the Virginia Museum of Fine Arts, established in 1936 as the first state museum. The museum created a new type of "dynamic" display—the Artmobile, galleries on wheels that carry priceless exhibits of art to areas not served by the state's network of fifty-one associate museums. This unique project is now being copied by museums all over the world. The museum also has a notable million-dollar Theater of the Performing Arts.

In the 1960s the museum embarked on a bold $5,600,000 expansion program financed by state appropriation, probably the most significant state contribution to fine art in the nation to that time. New construction included a breathtaking entrance portico and a waterfall flanked by sculpture gardens.

Other Richmond museums are the Valentine Museum, the Richmond Academy of Medicine, and Battle Abbey.

In the vicinity of Richmond are many interesting attractions for visitors. It was the mayor of Petersburg, a town about twenty-five miles (forty kilometers) to the south of Richmond, who is said to have been the first person to bestow on Washington the title "Father of His Country." Also at Petersburg are memories of its pillaging in the Revolutionary War and especially the key role played by the city in the Civil War. Here may be seen the remains of one of the most fantastic actions of the war. A regiment of miners from Pennsylvania burrowed under the Confederate lines for 500 feet (152.4 meters). In this tunnel 8,000 pounds (about 3,628 kilograms) of gunpowder set off an explosion that stunned both sides and killed many Confederate soldiers. It blew a crater 30 feet (about 9 meters) deep stretching for 135 feet (41.2 meters). Federal forces were driven into the pit and virtually massacred. The defeat may have been a key reason in the Union failure to take Richmond in 1864.

Other historic spots near Richmond are Studley House, which is the birthplace of Patrick Henry, Seven Pines National Cemetery, and the little brick schoolhouse where Thomas Jefferson received some of his early education. As a boy, he inscribed his name on the building's wall.

THREE SIGNIFICANT PLACES

Williamsburg, Jamestown, and Yorktown, all on a small peninsula of land between the James and the York rivers, have been described as "the three most significant places in our heritage."

The area is now Colonial National Historical Park. The ruined church remains, with three-foot-thick (about one meter) broken walls of handmade brick that once surrounded the structure built in 1639 on the spot where John Rolfe and Pocahontas had been married in 1614. The actual earrings worn by the Indian princess may still be seen in the visitor center of the national park, along with other relics and exhibits of colonial times. America's first factory has been reproduced in the Glass House, where glassware is made just as it was in 1680. A five-mile (eight-kilometer) wilderness trail through the forests provides a vivid example of what the region was like when the colonists first arrived.

Jamestown They rest quietly now, those pioneer colonists of Jamestown; the ancient trees have wrapped themselves around their tombs. Only a vine-covered church tower remains as a reminder of all their accomplishments, and even their land itself would have been washed away except for a sea wall built in 1901. The rest of the earliest portion of Jamestown consists of only a fragment of a foundation, the remnant of a street, an ancient hedgerow, or property ditch, and some other scattered relics. No one lives in the city now.

Nearby, the Commonwealth of Virginia has built a fascinating reproduction of earlier days called Jamestown Festival Park. Here is a full-scale reconstruction of triangular James Fort and its eighteen wattle-and-daub buildings, thrown up in 1607 to guard against Indians and Spaniards. There are displays in a New World and an Old War pavilion, and a reconstruction of Powhatan's lodge. Full-scale reproductions of three ships, *Susan Constant* (100 tons/90.7 metric tons), *Godspeed* (40 tons/36.3 metric tons), and *Discovery* (20 tons/ 18.1 metric tons) cause visitors to marvel that people were willing to risk their lives and cross the mighty ocean in such tiny vessels. These are anchored in the James River near the Fort.

Williamsburg As Christmas approaches in restored colonial Williamsburg, the great yule log is brought in. Carolers in colonial costume stroll from window to window with their message of song. The traditional Christmas guns are fired. The governor himself presides over a Christmas harpsichord concert in the candlelit hall of the magnificent Governor's Mansion. Feasts of Virginia ham, Sally Lunn bread, roasted Virginia oysters, fragrant mince pies, and flaming plum pudding weigh down the groaning board, and those who feast carefully tie yard-square napkins about their necks. Craftsmen in different shops hurry to finish their work in hand printing, blacksmithing, wigmaking, hand leather tooling, or candle making in

Duke of Gloucester Street in colonial Williamsburg, Virginia

time for Christmas. Coachmen in tricornered hats guide their horses down Duke of Gloucester Street.

All this is as it took place in seventeenth-century Virginia. Nowhere else in the world is it possible to go back so completely and authentically to another time as in Colonial Williamsburg.

This amazing accomplishment has cost more than $77,000,000 and the extremely painstaking work of hundreds of experts over many decades, as well as the devotion of people famous and unknown to make the unusual dream come true. The dream was that of the Reverend Dr. W.A.R. Goodwin, who fired the imagination of John D. Rockefeller, Jr. Rockefeller saw in it a great educational project with the aim "that the future may learn from the past."

Most of Williamsburg is restored to the way it looked at its peak as the fashionable social capital of Virginia. Thirty-seven buildings, containing 230 exhibition rooms, may now be seen just as they once looked. Some were still standing when the restoration began; others, such as the historic Governor's Mansion (burned during its use as a Revolutionary hospital), had to be carefully rebuilt on the original foundations.

To restore the mansion, an old picture was carefully studied, as were three hundred pages of original writings on the building. Complete inventories of the contents of the building under three

The Governor's Mansion, Williamsburg

Yorktown Battlefield in the Colonial National Historical Park.

different governors were available, so the mansion could be furnished almost exactly as it was in its glory. The superb gardens, including the vast maze, have been carefully recreated.

The old jail was still standing, and was simply restored. Here the infamous pirate Blackbeard was once held, and nine of his pirate crew were executed on Gallows Road.

Fascinating, too, at Williamsburg are the colonial craft shops: milling, spinning and weaving, millinery, bakery, apothecary, bootmaking, and many others. In these, workers ply their trades just as in the old days along Duke of Gloucester Street, sometimes called "the most historic street in all America."

Other interesting portions of Williamsburg are the Abby Aldrich Rockefeller Folk Art Collection, the Craft House, and the historic College of William and Mary, with its Wren Building, the oldest academic building in the United States.

Yorktown Jamestown and Williamsburg are connected by the Colonial Parkway, which also ties in the third historic site included in the Colonial National Historical Park—Yorktown. The town itself is almost surrounded by Yorktown Battlefield, where the remains of British fortifications and the camping places of the Americans may still be seen. The Visitor Center has many interesting exhibits of the Revolution. A tour of the battleground may include the headquarters locations of such leaders as General Friedrich von Steuben, the Marquis de Lafayette, General Jean Baptiste Rochambeau, and George Washington. On the edge of the battlefield is Moore House where the Articles of Capitulation (surrender) were written. Yorktown National Cemetery contains the graves of 2,204 American dead.

FOUR FOR THE ROADS

The metropolitan area centered at Hampton Roads includes four major Virginia communities—Norfolk, Portsmouth, Newport News, and Hampton.

NORFOLK

Norfolk is now the largest city in Virginia and completely modern, with one of the most complete civic centers in the country, including a nine-million-dollar city hall. However, the influence of the sea and of its long history still are strong.

Old St. Paul's Church was one of the few buildings to survive the battles of 1776; in its aged walls may still be seen one of the cannonballs embedded there during the British cannonades in the War of 1812. The Adam Thoroughgood House is believed to be the oldest English-built brick residence in the nation.

One of the great shrines in Norfolk is the General Douglas MacArthur Memorial, housed in what once was the city hall. Here is one of the world's finest collections of twentieth-century war implements, as well as the tomb of one of America's most famous generals.

Other interesting displays are to be seen at the Chrysler Museum; magnificent wood carvings and a fabulous oriental art collection are part of the collection of the Hermitage Foundation. At the Myers House visitors can enjoy the elegance of a home belonging to an eighteenth-century merchant prince.

A special air-conditioned bus takes visitors on a guided tour of Norfolk's naval base and naval air station. Norfolk is also noted for its Gardens-by-the-Sea. Here in the spring 250,000 azaleas bloom, along with other spring blossoms, and a queen is crowned for the International Azalea Festival.

The summer playground of the area is famous Virginia Beach, with its 2 miles (3.2 kilometers) of boardwalk and 8 miles (12.9 kilometers) of beach.

PORTSMOUTH

Portsmouth is connected with Norfolk by two toll tunnels and two bridges. The Portsmouth section of the naval complex is known as Norfolk Naval Shipyard in Portsmouth. A Naval Shipyard Museum displays thousands of navy items, along with pictures and models of ships. Portsmouth also has the oldest naval hospital in the United States. Many notable historic homes are still standing in Portsmouth.

Near Portsmouth is the Dismal Swamp, once the eerie refuge of desperate fugitives. Boat tours through this unusual area may be arranged.

NEWPORT NEWS

Newport News, named for Sir Christopher Newport, is the third of the great cities on Hampton Roads. It is noted for two unique museums. The Mariners Museum is surrounded by an 880-acre (356-hectare) game sanctuary. In the museum are vast collections of ship models and miniature ships, ships' instruments and other maritime exhibits. One of the most fascinating displays is that of the figureheads from many ships, ranging from saucy mermaids to the prim figure of a captain's wife with parasol and prayer book. A huge golden eagle figurehead spreads his wings across most of a room.

The War Memorial Museum of Virginia holds one of the most complete collections of materials on the World Wars and the Korean War. A relic of other wars, Fort Monroe frowns out over the entrance to Chesapeake Bay and Hampton Roads. Famous prisoners held over the years at Fort Monroe included Chief Black Hawk and Jefferson Davis.

HAMPTON

Hampton, founded in 1610, is the fourth major city in the Norfolk metropolitan area. Because Jamestown is not now occupied, Hampton claims to be the oldest continually inhabited English settlement in the New World. Syms-Eaton Museum at Hampton honors the names of the men who started the first free schools in the United States—Benjamin Syms and Thomas Eaton; here are Indian relics and mementos of old Hampton. Hampton Institute, Langley Air Force Base, the National Aeronautics and Space Administration, and Big Bethel Battlefield are other points of interest in the Hampton area.

THE REST OF THE EAST

Fairfax County is one of the largest areas in the country under a single local government. The biggest city in the Virginia portion of the Washington, D.C., metropolitan area is Alexandria, begun in 1732 by a group of Scottish merchants. George Washington helped to survey the streets.

The Masons are an international fraternal organization with a long and colorful history. Washington is remembered by his fellow Masons in the George Washington Masonic National Memorial at Alexandria. This startling 333-foot-high (101.5 meters) building with carillon and organ was built at a cost of five million dollars with contributions from three million Masons all over the country.

Three wars all spared Alexandria, so that homes of many famous people are still to be seen there. One of the most unusual houses was the narrow "Flounder" house, built that way to avoid taxes. In Christ Church is the brass and crystal chandelier presented by vestryman George Washington. On the streets of Alexandria the *Gazette,* the oldest daily newspaper in the country, can still be purchased. Here also is the old apothecary shop where Martha Washington bought castor oil by the quart.

There are no incorporated cities or towns in Arlington County, but its population is about 170,000. Within its boundaries are some of the nation's most historic sites, as well as the vast Pentagon Building, the largest office building in the world, and busy Washington National Airport.

Arlington National Cemetery is the largest and best known of all our national cemeteries. More than 119,000 military persons and other national figures are buried there. Among the most famous of those who rest in Arlington are Presidents John F. Kennedy and William Howard Taft. Other famous names include General John J. Pershing, who lies among his soldiers at his own request in a less-prominent part of the cemetery, Robert Todd Lincoln, William Jennings Bryan, Admirals Robert E. Perry and Richard E. Byrd, General George C. Marshall, and John Foster Dulles, the Secretary of State under President Eisenhower.

Pierre Charles L'Enfant, designer of Washington, is buried in a grave overlooking the city. Polish patriot-musician Jan Paderewski is buried in Arlington. The Arlington Monument to the Confederate Dead was a gift of the Daughters of the Confederacy to symbolize a reunited people. The mast of the battleship *Maine* stands on high ground, a memorial to the sailors who lost their lives when it was sunk.

The Arlington Memorial Amphitheater, dedicated by President Woodrow Wilson in 1920, was built as a memorial to the Army, Navy, and Marine Corps dead and as a gathering place for those who attend Memorial Day and other services.

82

Nearby is one of most hallowed shrines in the United States—the Tomb of the Unknown Soldiers. Great pains were taken to be sure that the World War I hero buried beneath the simple impressive monument was truly "known but to God." The body was placed in its present resting place after being brought from Washington in one of the most celebrity-filled processions of all time. Later, more bodies were added to the shrine to represent the unknown dead of more recent wars.

In the cemetery area is the Custis-Lee Mansion National Memorial. When General Lafayette visited here in 1824 he said the view was unequaled in all the world. The stately house overlooking Washington was built by Martha Washington's grandson, George Washington Parke Custis. His daughter married Robert E. Lee and the beautiful interior now has many mementos of the Washington and Lee families.

An even more famous mansion is Mount Vernon, the estate so beloved by George Washington. In 1853 Ann Pamela Cunningham organized the Mount Vernon Ladies' Association of the Union to buy and restore the historic house and grounds. Today it is much as it was in Washington's day and is considered a good expression of his character. In spite of his tremendous public works, it might be said

Changing of the guard at the Tomb of the Unknown Soldiers.

that Mount Vernon and his family were Washington's principal interests. Some of the happiest pages from his diary were written about the plantation life here. Among the interesting contents of the home are the harpsichord Washington imported for his step-daughter, Nelly, at a cost of a thousand pounds sterling, most of his books, and the key to the French Bastille presented by Lafayette.

George and Martha Washington are buried in a simple tomb on the grounds, having spurned the elaborate tomb prepared for them in the national capitol building. Thirty-one other members of the Washington family are buried in the cemetery, at what is now George Washington Birthplace National Monument near Oak Grove. The mansion in the monument is not the actual birthplace but a reproduction of a typical Virginia plantation.

Fredericksburg has some of the finest homes remaining from colonial times, including Mary Washington's house, where she gave her blessing to her son before he went to the Presidency, and Kenmore, often called one of the best restorations in the country. Also at Fredericksburg is the law office of James Monroe, now a museum where may be seen the desk on which the President wrote the Monroe Doctrine.

Fredericksburg and Spotsylvania National Military Park commemorate some of the heaviest fighting ever experienced on this continent. The park includes portions of four battlefields and the Fredericksburg National Cemetery. Almost thirteen thousand of those buried there were of unknown identity. Nearby is the Stonewall Jackson Memorial Shrine, at the plantation office where Jackson died of pneumonia after being wounded. It was here that he murmured while dying, "Let us cross over the river, and rest under the shade of the trees."

The Indians called Virginia's lower (eastern) peninsula Accawmacke; today one of its counties is Accomack, taken from the Indian name. The picturesque Eastern Shore is said to be a "world apart." One of the most exciting events of the region is the annual Pony Penning Day. Wild horses have lived so long on the not very nutritious grasses of Chincoteague Island that they are now stunted to slightly more than pony size. Each year they are rounded up and forced to swim the inlet. Foals are branded and many ponies auctioned. Chincoteague Ocean Beach on Assateague Island is a part of the Assateague National Seashore.

On the Eastern Shore may be seen many houses built in the seventeenth and early eighteenth centuries. Tangier Island, in the middle of lower Chesapeake Bay, has about one thousand inhabitants who speak with an Old English accent and follow many customs of their ancestors. The streets of Tangier are not wide enough for automobiles.

INTERIOR CITIES

Roanoke, first settled in 1740, is the leading commercial and industrial center of western Virginia. In the city are manufactured fabricated steel, railroad cars, electronic equipment, fiberglass boats, fabrics, clothing, wood furniture, and flour. It lies in a cup-shaped area between the Allegheny Mountains and the Blue Ridge. It has no connection with the Roanoke colony that disappeared in 1591 from Roanoke Island off the coast of North Carolina.

Rising one thousand feet (just over three hundred meters) within the city is Mill Mountain, topped by Roanoke's famous neon star, said to be the largest in the world. The city-owned mountain, with a magnificent view, is a park with the only children's zoo in the state. Roanoke's Transportation Museum displays a collection of boats, locomotives, airplanes, and antique cars.

Near Roanoke is Booker T. Washington National Monument. On the two hundred-acre (about eighty-one-hectare) plantation where this leader was born as a slave is a replica of his boyhood cabin. The spring from which the family took its water still flows. The visitor center has exhibits showing Washington's life.

The tobacco town of Lynchburg perches on the bluffs of the James River. It boasts the largest dark tobacco market in the South and one of the largest anywhere. There the strange chant of the tobacco auctioneer rings out. The town was founded by a seventeen-year-old Quaker, John Lynch, in 1757. The striking Lynchburg War

Memorial looks out over the city and is reached by an impressive approach of stairs and terraces. At nearby Brookneal is the simple tomb of Patrick Henry on the grounds of his last home, Red Hill.

Even today Charlottesville seems to be dominated by memories of its most famous citizen, Thomas Jefferson—the estate he created, the university he founded and designed.

The University of Virginia, with its handsome red brick buildings, sweeping vistas, serpentine walls only one brick thick (another Jefferson innovation), and its ancient trees, has long been one of the most admired campuses in the United States. Its Brooks Museum offers interesting displays, and the university rooms occupied by Woodrow Wilson and Edgar Allan Poe as students are open to the public.

The Thomas Jefferson Memorial Foundation has restored and maintains Monticello. The estate was built by Jefferson with materials, even nails, made on the spot. The inventions and devices Jefferson installed in the interior make it one of the unique houses of this country. Shadwell, Jefferson's birthplace near Monticello, has been reconstructed.

Ash Lawn, home of another President, James Monroe, is also open to the public. It contains many of Monroe's possessions.

Charlottesville is noted for its many monuments, including those of Stonewall Jackson on his horse Little Sorrell, Robert E. Lee, and the explorers Lewis and Clark. There is also a George Rogers Clark Memorial.

At Barboursville, in Madison Cemetery, are the graves of James and Dolley Madison.

Woodrow Wilson's birthplace in Staunton is now a national shrine. A different kind of "shrine" is the McCormick Reaper Museum, where the first reaper is displayed. General U.S. Grant allowed the Staunton Military Band to keep its instruments at the end of the war. When he visited the city as President, the band gave him the first welcome he had ever received in the South. Near Staunton is a unique formation known as Natural Chimneys. Here an unusual jousting tournament is said to be America's oldest sporting event in continuous operation.

THE MOUNTAIN SWEEP

Two of the world's most unusual roads snake their way along the crests of the Blue Ridge—the Blue Ridge Parkway and connecting Skyline Drive. About 300 square miles (777 square kilometers) of the most beautiful scenery of the Blue Ridge are found in Shenandoah National Park—still an unspoiled wilderness playground. The Shenandoah Valley is a fertile checkerboard of green and gold.

Natural wonders of the region include famed Luray Caverns and Shenandoah Caverns. Another natural formation, farther to the south, is Natural Bridge. Thomas Jefferson bought the bridge for twenty shillings from the Indians.

The oldest Virginia city west of the Blue Ridge is Winchester, sometimes known as the Apple Capital of the world. Here was George Washington's first office, as well as wartime headquarters of General Jackson and later of General Sheridan during the Civil War.

Two of the most famous comrades in arms have found their final resting place at Lexington. Robert E. Lee's grave lies beneath the chapel of Washington and Lee University, under the famous recumbent statue of the General. A bronze statue marks the grave of Stonewall Jackson in the Presbyterian Cemetery. The only home he ever owned is now restored as a memorial to him.

The Museum of Virginia Military Institute at Lexington has many mementos of war and of wartime figures, including Jackson, George Marshall, and George S. Patton.

Covington is surrounded by Warm Springs, Sweet Springs, and Lick mountains. Nearby Falling Springs is higher than Niagara Falls.

One of the attractions of Covington is a humpback covered bridge, the only one of this construction remaining in the country. Crow Tavern at Covington once overflowed with so many travelers that the tavern rules prohibited more than five persons in a bed. Warm meals were advertised at $12\frac{2}{3}$ cents and cold ones at $10\frac{1}{2}$ cents.

New Castle was noted for its fair. In 1737 the sponsors of the fair announced "that 20 horses or mares do run round a three-mile course for a prize of five pounds . . . that a violin be played for by 20 fiddlers . . . they are all to play together and each a different tune

. . . that handsome entertainment be provided for the subscribers and their wives; and such of them as are not so happy as to have wives may treat any other lady . . . that a quire of ballads be sung by a number of songsters, all of them to have liquor sufficient to clear their wind pipes."

Radford is the gateway to the Virginia highlands and New River Valley. Here Mary Draper Ingles made a famous escape from Indian captivity. Here also the Ingles Ferry provided a link in the Great Road from Philadelphia to Louisville.

The best known of all Virginia state activities is a world-famous Barter Theater at Abingdon. It was founded by a group of New York actors during the Great Depression. Theatergoers without money could bring a glass of jelly, a ham, or another worthwhile item to barter for a ticket. Today the Barter Theater is the Virginia State Theater—the only state theater in the country.

Bristol, Virginia, is one of a pair of twin cities on the Virginia-Tennessee line, which runs down the middle of State Street. The Tennessee side is also called Bristol. The city is now a principal industrial center. Interesting Bristol Caverns are nearby.

West of Gate City is an unusual natural tunnel 100 feet (about 30 meters) in diameter and 900 feet (about 275 meters) long, carved through the rock by wind and water. It is used as a railroad tunnel.

Big Stone Gap is the home of Southwest Virginia Museum, a collection of Indian relics, war mementos, and agricultural and other implements. The town still remembers the time its most famous resident, author John Fox, Jr., married famed light-opera star Fritzi Scheff after a twenty-four-hour courtship and brought her home to Big Stone Gap. The dazzling, bejeweled favorite of two continents found the hills not as romantic as her husband had written they were, and soon left both them and him.

Breaks Interstate Park in the Cumberlands, shared with Kentucky, and Cumberland Gap National Historical Park preserve some of America's most historic wilderness area. Through this region came some of the earliest western pioneers. And because of them Virginia came to be called the "Mother of the Frontier," as well as the "Mother of English Settlement in America."

Handy Reference Section

Instant Facts

Official name—Commonwealth of Virginia
Became 10th state—June 25, 1788
Capital—Richmond, founded 1737
Nickname—The Old Dominion
State motto—*Sic Semper Tyrannis* (Thus Ever to Tyrants)
State flower and state tree—American Dogwood
State song—*Carry Me Back to Old Virginia,* by James A. Bland
Area—40,815 square miles (105,710 kilometers)
Rank in area—36th
Shoreline—3,315 miles (5,335 kilometers)
Coastline—112 miles (180 kilometers)
Greatest length (north to south)—209 miles (336 kilometers)
Greatest width (east to west)—452 miles (727 kilometers)
Geographic center—5 miles (8 kilometers) southwest of Buckingham
Highest point—5,729 feet (1,746 meters), Mount Rogers
Lowest point—Sea level
Population—5,229,000 (1980 projection)
Population density—128.1 per square mile (49.5 per square kilometer) (1980 projection)
Rank in density—16th
Population center—In Powhatan County, 5.2 miles (8.4 kilometers) northwest of Powhatan
Birthrate—15 per 1,000
Principal cities   (1975 est.)

Norfolk	286,694
Richmond	232,652
Arlington (County)	174,284 (1970 census)
Virginia Beach	213,954
Newport News	138,760
Hampton	125,013
Portsmouth	108,674
Alexandria	105,220

You Have a Date with History

1497—John Cabot explores region
c. 1580—Spanish missionaries establish base on Aquia Creek
1607—Jamestown founded
1609—John Smith returns to England
1614—John Rolfe marries Pocahontas

1618—First American university chartered
1619—House of Burgesses established
1622—Opechancanough's massacre, March 22
1634—Benjamin Syms endows first free school in colonies, Hampton
1674—Nathaniel Bacon's rebellion
1693—College of William and Mary chartered
1699—Capital moves to Williamsburg
1732—George Washington born, February 22
1737—Richmond founded
1743—Thomas Jefferson born, April 13
1759—George Washington marries Martha Custis
1763—French and Indian War ends
1773—Virginia Committee of Correspondence formed
1776—Virginia declares itself a free state
1778—Virginia forbids slave trade
1779—Richmond becomes capital
1781—Lord Cornwallis surrenders to Americans, Yorktown
1788—Virginia becomes a state, June
1789—First Jewish congregation established in Virginia
1790—Richmond-Westham canal opens
1792—Original capitol completed
1792—Kentucky becomes a separate state
1799—George Washington dies, December 14
1812—Dismal Swamp canal opens
1813—First steamboats in Virginia waters
1818—University of Virginia chartered
1826—Thomas Jefferson dies, July 4
1831—Cyrus McCormick invents the reaper
1831—Chesterfield Railroad opens
1831—James Monroe dies, July 4
1836—James Madison dies, June 28
1861—Virginia secedes from United States, April 17
1861—Richmond becomes Confederate capital, May 29
1862—*Monitor-Merrimac* battle
1863—West Virginia becomes separate state
1865—Robert E. Lee surrenders at Appomattox
1869—Reconstruction constitution approved
1870—Virginia again a sovereign state
1894—Maryland boundary settled
1902—New constitution
1903—North Carolina boundary settled
1917—United States enters World War I
1918—Influenza epidemic claims 11,641 Virginia lives
1924—Woodrow Wilson dies, February 3
1927—State government reorganized
1932—Harry F. Byrd becomes United States Senator

1941—United States enters World War II
1959—First Virginia schools integrated, February 2
1966—Space Radiation Effects Laboratory opens
1969—A. Linwood Holton becomes first Republican governor in 100 years
1970—New constitution

Governors of the Commonwealth of Virginia

Patrick Henry, 1776-1779
Thomas Jefferson, 1779-1781
William Fleming, 1781
Thomas Nelson, Jr., 1781
Benjamin Harrison, 1781-1784
Patrick Henry, 1784-1786
Edmund Randolph, 1786-1788
Beverly Randolph, 1788-1791
Henry Lee, 1791-1794
Robert Brooke, 1794-1796
Hardin Burnely, 1796
James Wood, 1796-1799
J. Pendleton, 1799
James Monroe, 1799-1802
John Page, 1802-1805
William H. Cabell, 1805-1808
John Tyler, 1808-1811
George William Smith, 1811
James Monroe, 1811
Peyton Randolph, 1811-1812
James Barbour, 1812-1814
Wilson Carry Nicholas, 1814-1816
James Patton Preston, 1816-1819
Thomas Mann Randolph, 1819-1822
James Pleasants, Jr., 1822-1825
John Tyler, Jr., 1825-1827
William Branch Giles, 1827-1830
John Floyd, 1830-1834
Littleton Waller Tazewell, 1834-1836
Wyndham Robertson, 1836-1837
David Campbell, 1837-1840
Thomas Walker Gilmer, 1840-1841
John Mercer Patton, 1841
John Rutherford, 1841-1842
John Munford Gregory, 1843-1843
James McDowell, 1843-1846
William Smith, 1846-1849

John Buchanan Floyd, 1849-1852
Joseph Johnson, 1852-1856
Henry Alexander Wise, 1856-1860
John Letcher, 1860-1864
William Smith, 1864-1865
Francis Harrison Pierpont, 1865-1868
Henry Horatio Wells, 1868-1869
Gilbert Carlton Walker, 1869-1874
James Lawson Kemper, 1874-1878
Frederick William Mackey Holliday,
   1878-1882
William Evelyn Cameron, 1882-1886
Fitzhugh Lee, 1886-1890
Philip Watkins McKinney, 1890-1894
Charles Triplett O'Ferrall, 1894-1898
James Hoge Tyler, 1898-1902
Andrew Jackson Montague, 1902-1906
Claude Augustus Swanson, 1906-1910
William Hodges Mann, 1910-1914
Henry Carter Stuart, 1914-1918
Westmoreland Davis, 1918-1922
Elbert Lee Trinkle, 1922-1926
Harry Flood Byrd, 1926-1930
John Garland Pollard, 1930-1934
George Campbell Perry, 1934-1938
James Hubert Price, 1938-1942
Colgate Whitehead Darden, Jr.,
   1942-1946
William Munford Tuck, 1946-1950
John Stewart Battle, 1950-1954
Thomas Bahnson Stanley, 1954-1958
James Lindsay Almond, Jr., 1958-1962
Albertis Sydney Harrison, Jr., 1962-1966
Mills E. Godwin, Jr., 1966-1970
A. Linwood Holton, 1970—1974
Mills E. Godwin, Jr., 1974-

Index

92

94

PICTURE CREDITS

ABOUT THE AUTHOR

With the publication of his first book for school use when he was twenty, **Allan Carpenter** began a career as an author that has spanned more than 135 books. After teaching in the public schools of Des Moines, Mr. Carpenter began his career as an educational publisher at the age of twenty-one when he founded the magazine *Teachers Digest.* In the field of educational periodicals, he was responsible for many innovations. During his many years in publishing, he has perfected a highly organized approach to handling large volumes of factual material: after extensive traveling and having collected all possible materials, he systematically reviews and organizes everything. From his apartment high in Chicago's John Hancock Building, Allan recalls, "My collection and assimilation of materials on the states and countries began before the publication of my first book." Allan is the founder of Carpenter Publishing House and of Infordata International, Inc., publishers of *Issues in Education* and *Index to U. S. Government Periodicals.* When he is not writing or traveling, his principal avocation is music. He has been the principal bassist of many symphonies, and he managed the country's leading non-professional symphony for twenty-five years.